EASY PIANO

SIMPLE JAZZ SONGS

THE EASIEST EASY PIANO SONGS

ISBN 978-1-70511-097-3

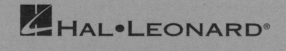

HAL•LEONARD®

Visit Hal Leonard Online at
www.halleonard.com

Contact us:
Hal Leonard
7777 West Bluemound Road
Milwaukee, WI 53213
Email: info@halleonard.com

In Europe, contact:
Hal Leonard Europe Limited
42 Wigmore Street
Marylebone, London, W1U 2RN
Email: info@halleonardeurope.com

In Australia, contact:
Hal Leonard Australia Pty. Ltd.
4 Lentara Court
Cheltenham, Victoria, 3192 Australia
Email: info@halleonard.com.au

AT LAST
from ORCHESTRA WIVES

Lyric by MACK GORDON
Music by HARRY WARREN

Slow Swing

mf

At

last_____ my love_____ has come a - long,_____

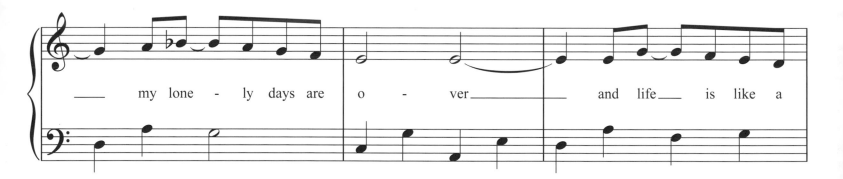

_____ my lone - ly days are o - ver_____ and life_____ is like a

song._____ At last_____

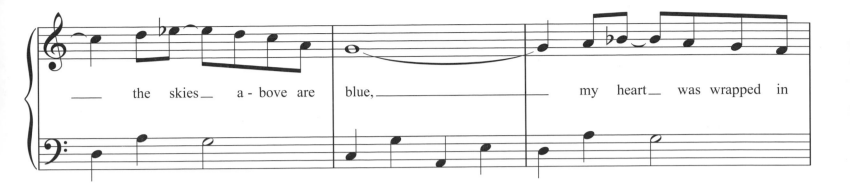

the skies___ a - bove are blue,_____ my heart___ was wrapped in

clo - ver_____ the night___ I looked at you._____

___ I found a dream that I can speak to_____ a dream that

I can call my own._____ I found a thrill to press my

6

cheek to, a thrill I've nev - er known. You

smiled_____ and then___ the spell was cast_____

___ and here___ we are in heav - en_____ for you are mine at

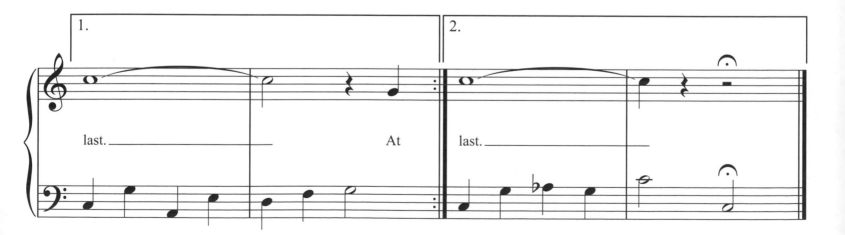

1.
last._____ At

2.
last._____

AS TIME GOES BY

from CASABLANCA

Words and Music by
HERMAN HUPFELD

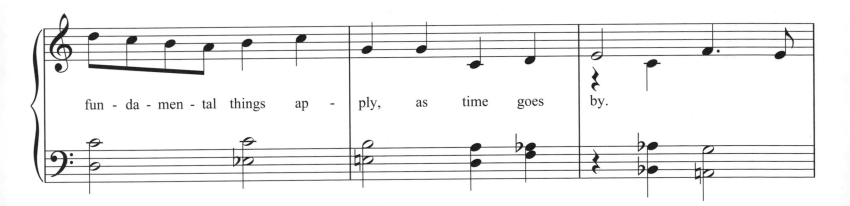

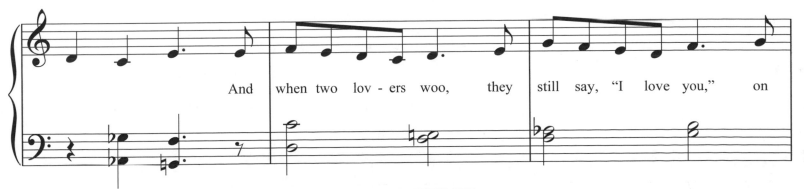

8

that you can re - ly; no mat - ter what the fu - ture

brings, as time goes by.

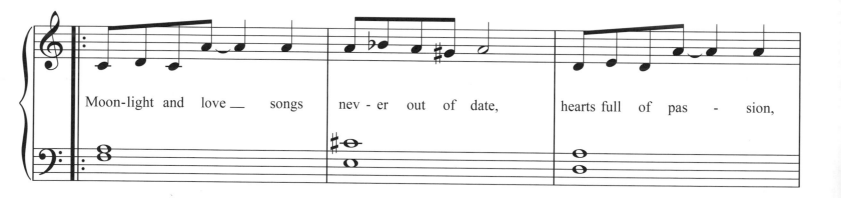

Moon-light and love __ songs nev - er out of date, hearts full of pas - sion,

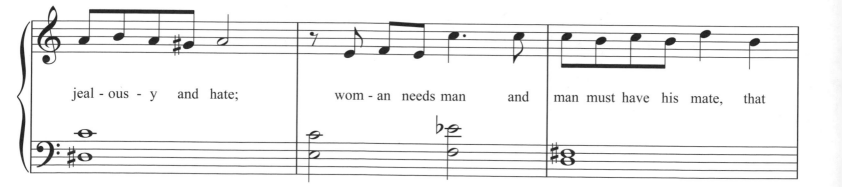

jeal - ous - y and hate; wom - an needs man and man must have his mate, that

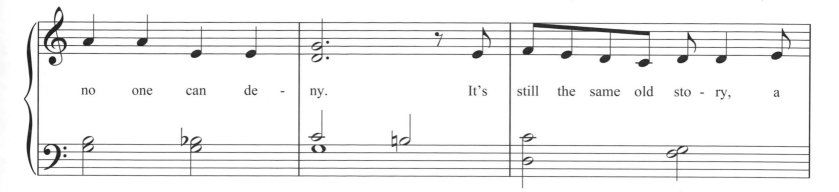

no one can de - ny.   It's still the same old sto - ry,   a

fight for love and glo - ry,   a case of do or die!   The

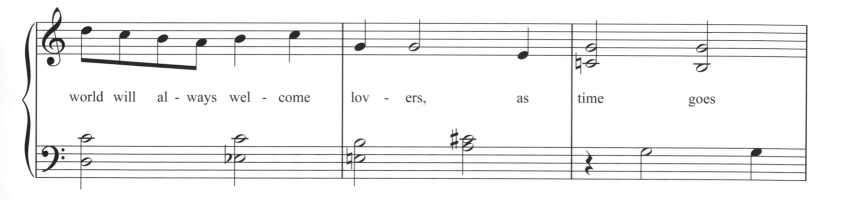

world will al - ways wel - come lov - ers,   as time goes

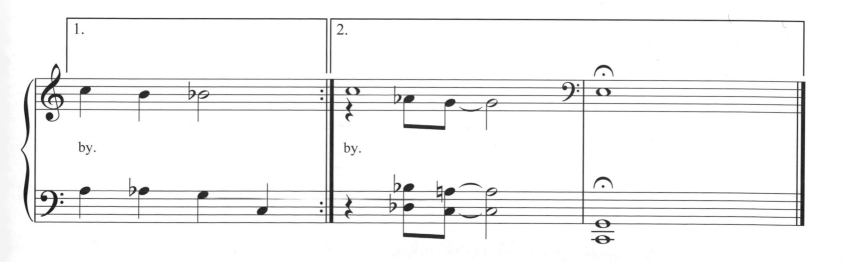

by.   by.

AUTUMN LEAVES

English lyric by JOHNNY MERCER
French lyric by JACQUES PREVERT
Music by JOSEPH KOSMA

Freely

Slowly

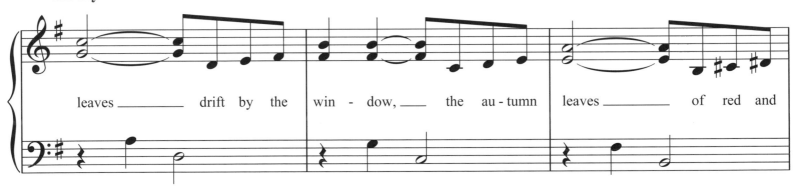

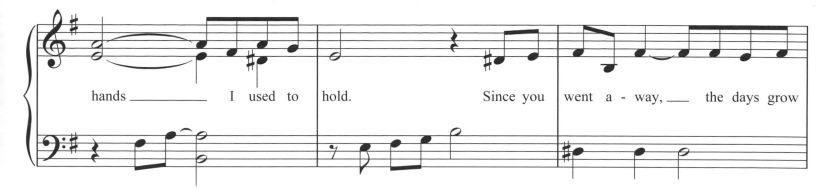

hands _____ I used to hold. Since you went a-way, ___ the days grow

long, _____ and soon I'll hear _____ old win-ter's song. But I
poco rit. *a tempo*

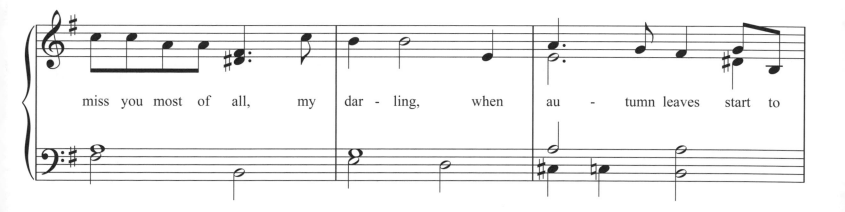

miss you most of all, my dar-ling, when au-tumn leaves start to

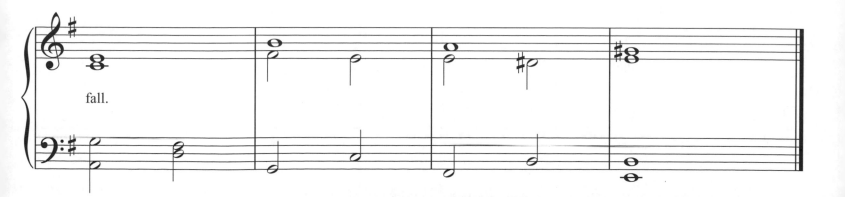

fall.

BEGIN THE BEGUINE

from JUBILEE

Words and Music by
COLE PORTER

Easy Latin feel

When they be - gin _____ the Be - guine _____ it

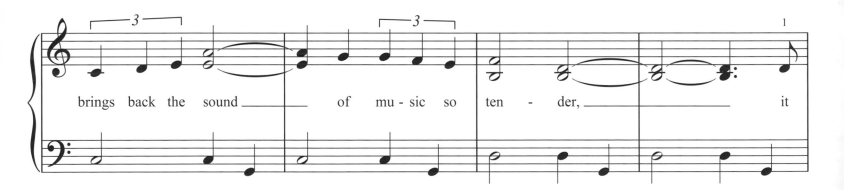

brings back the sound _____ of mu - sic so ten - der, _____ it

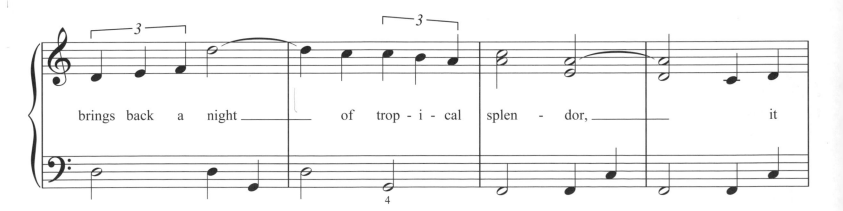

brings back a night _____ of trop - i - cal splen - dor, _____ it

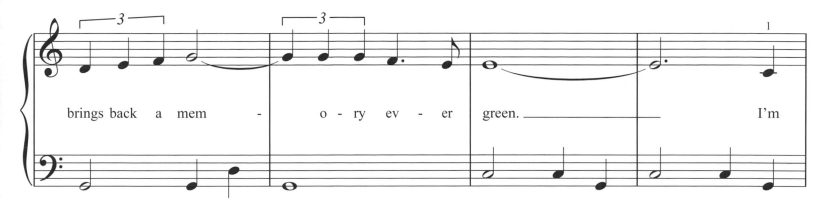

brings back a mem - o - ry ev - er green._____ I'm

with you once more _____ un - der the stars, _____ and

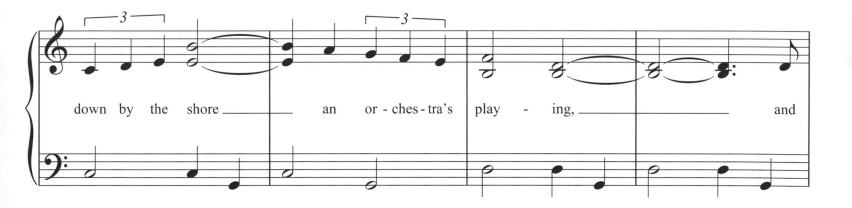

down by the shore _____ an or - ches - tra's play - ing, _____ and

e - ven the palms _____ seem to be sway - ing _____

14

when they be - gin _____ the Be - guine. _____ To

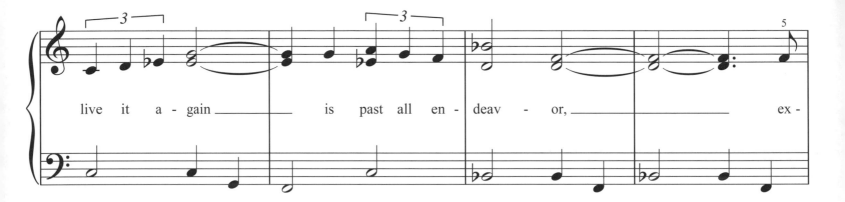

live it a - gain _____ is past all en - deav - or, _____ ex-

cept when that tune _____ clutch - es my heart, _____ and

there we are, swear - ing to love for - ev - er, and prom - is - ing

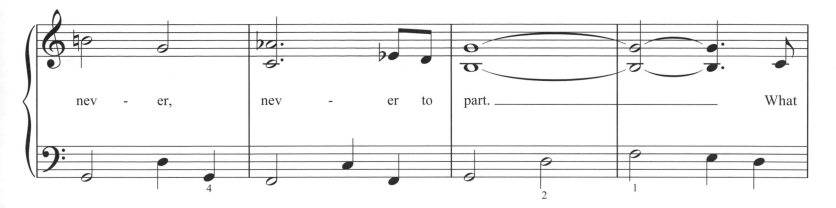

never, never er to part. _____ What

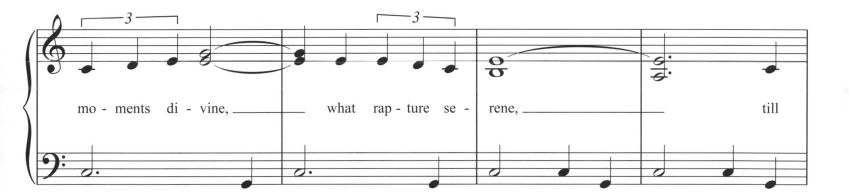

mo - ments di - vine, _____ what rap - ture se - rene, _____ till

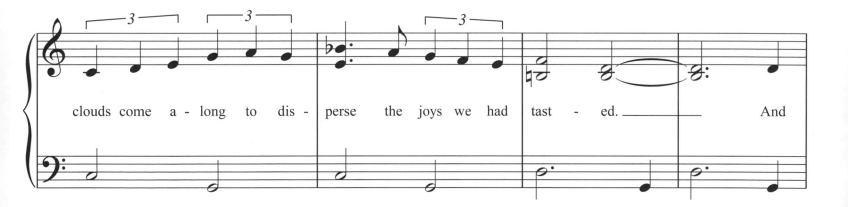

clouds come a - long to dis - perse the joys we had tast - ed. _____ And

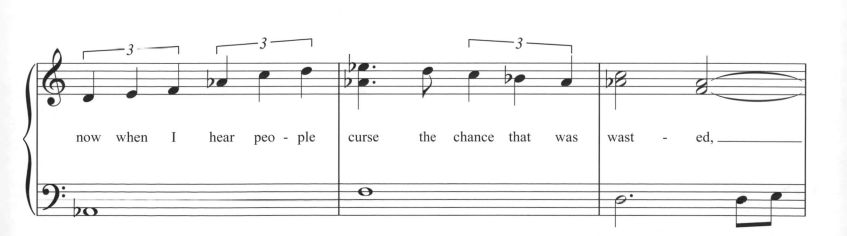

now when I hear peo - ple curse the chance that was wast - ed, _____

I know but too well _____ what they

mean. _____ So, don't let them be - gin _____

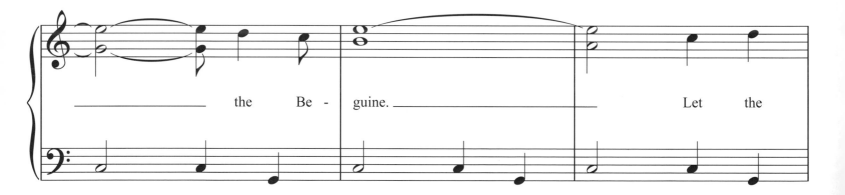

_____ the Be - guine. _____ Let the

love that was once a fire re - main an em - ber, _____

let it sleep like the dead de - sire I on - ly re -

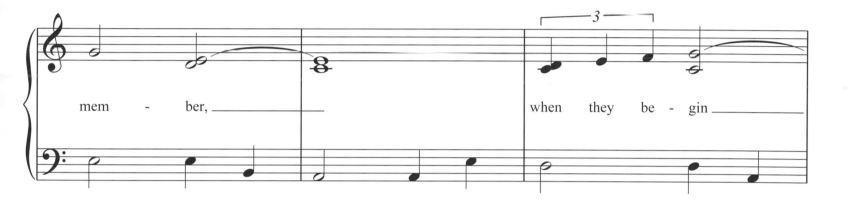

mem - ber, _____ when they be - gin _____

_____ the Be - guine. _____ Oh yes,

let them be - gin the Be - guine, make them play _____

till the stars that were there be - fore re - turn a -

bove you, till you whis - per to me once

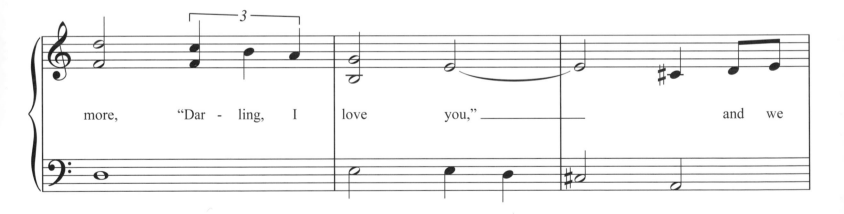

more, "Dar - ling, I love you," and we

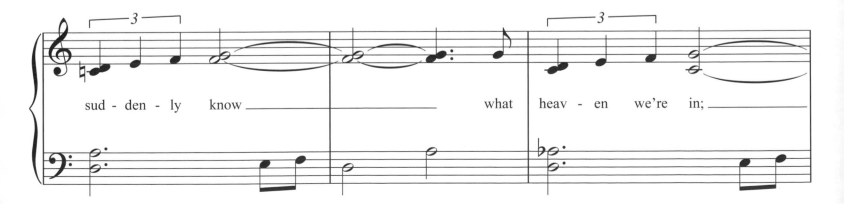

sud - den - ly know what heav - en we're in;

when they be - gin _____ the Be -

guine, _____ when they be - gin _____

the Be - guine.

rit.

THE BEST IS YET TO COME

Music by CY COLEMAN
Lyrics by CAROLYN LEIGH

Big Band Swing

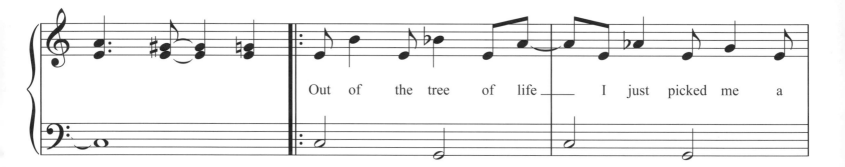

Out of the tree of life ___ I just picked me a

plum. ___ You came a - long and ev -

- 'ry - thing's start - in' to hum. ___

Still, it's a real good bet ____ the best is yet to come. ____

The best is yet to come, ____ and, babe, won't it be

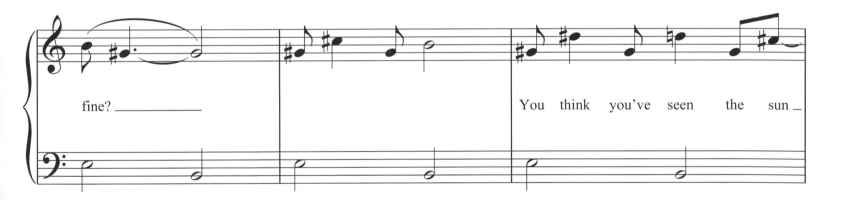

fine? ____ You think you've seen the sun ___

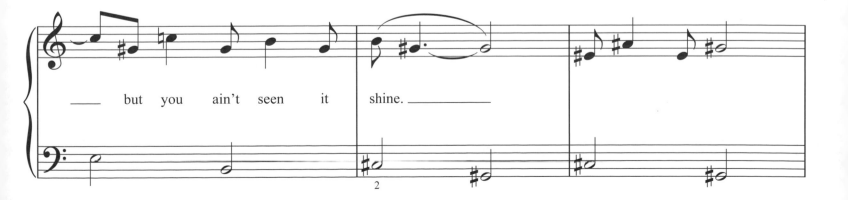

___ but you ain't seen it shine. ____

Wait till the warm-up's un - der - way, __ wait till our lips have met, __

__ wait till you see that sun - shine day. __

You ain't seen noth - in' yet! __ The best is yet to come, __

__ and, babe, won't it be fine? __

The best is yet to come, ___ come the day ___ you're mine.

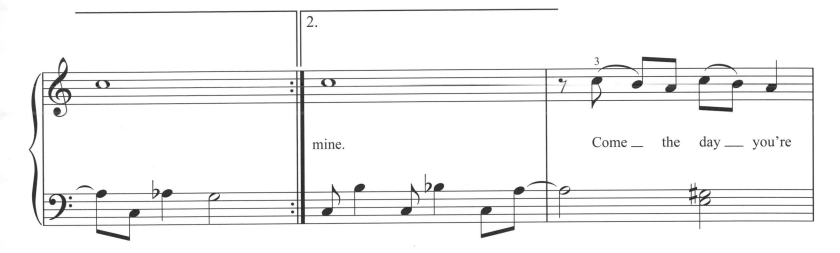

mine. Come ___ the day ___ you're

mine, I'm gon - na teach you to fly.

We've on - ly tast - ed the wine, we're gon - na drain the cup

24

dry.   Wait till   the   charms   are   ripe

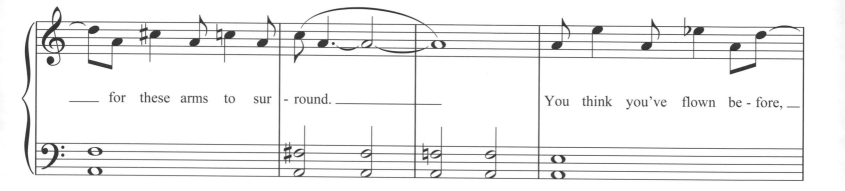

____ for these arms to sur - round. _____   You think you've flown be - fore, __

____ but you ain't left the ground. _____   Wait till you're locked in

my em - brace, __   wait till   I   draw you near. __

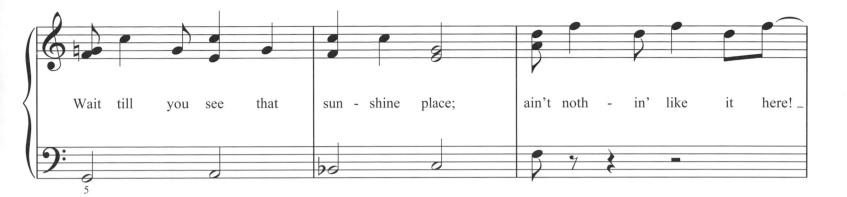

Wait till you see that sun - shine place; ain't noth - in' like it here! _

_ The best is yet to come _ and, babe, won't it be

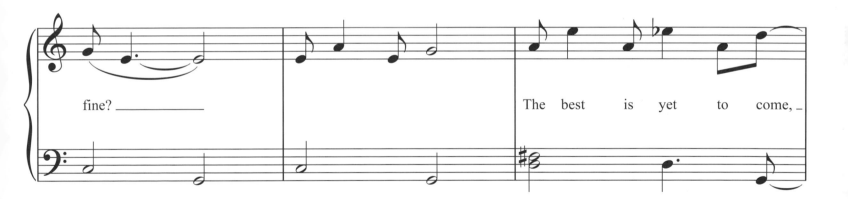

fine? _ The best is yet to come, _

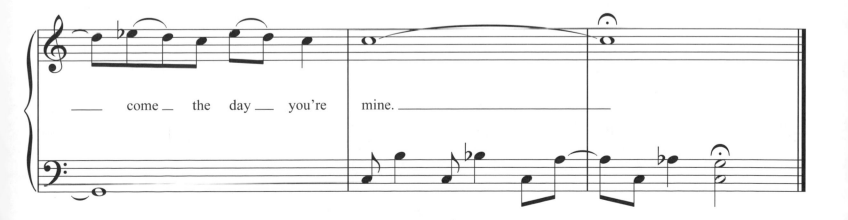

_ come _ the day _ you're mine. _

BLUE MOON

Music by RICHARD RODGERS
Lyrics by LORENZ HART

Freely

Once up-on a time, be - fore I took up smil - ing, I
Once up-on a time, my heart was just an or - gan; my

hat - ed the moon - light! Shad - ows of the night that
life had no mis - sion. Now that I have you, to

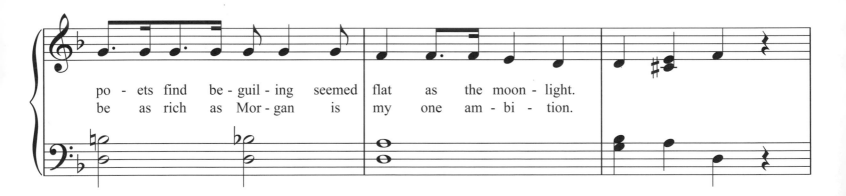

po - ets find be - guil - ing seemed flat as the moon - light.
be as rich as Mor - gan is my one am - bi - tion.

With no one to stay up for, I went to sleep at
Once I a - woke at sev - en, hat - ing the morn - ing

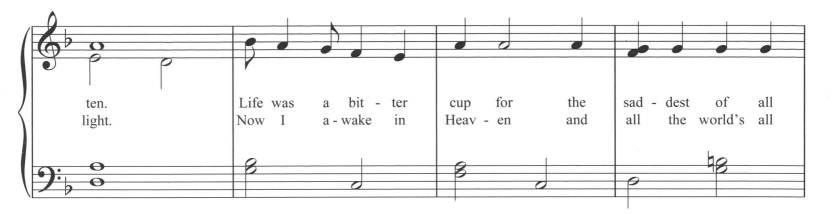

ten.
light.

Life was a bit-ter cup for the sad-dest of all
Now I a-wake in Heav-en and all the world's all

Relaxed Swing

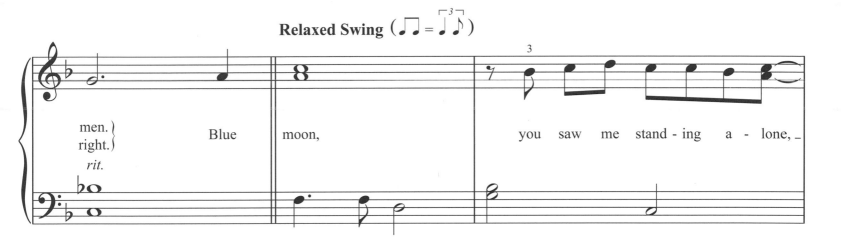

men.
right.

rit.

Blue moon, you saw me stand-ing a-lone,

with-out a dream in my heart,

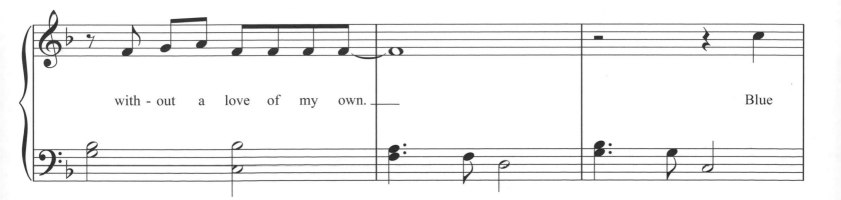

with-out a love of my own. Blue

moon, you knew just what I was there ____ for, _____

you heard me say-ing a prayer ____ for _____ some-one I real-ly could care _

____ for. And then there sud-den-ly ap-peared be -

fore me _____ the on-ly one my arms will ev-er hold. _____ I heard some-

bod - y whis- per, "Please a - dore me." _____ And when I looked, the moon had turned to

gold! Blue moon! Now I'm no long - er a - lone, _

_____ with-out a dream in my heart, _____ with-out a love of my own. _

1. _____ *rit.*

2. _____ *rit.*

BLUESETTE

Words by NORMAN GIMBEL
Music by JEAN THIELEMANS

Moderate Waltz

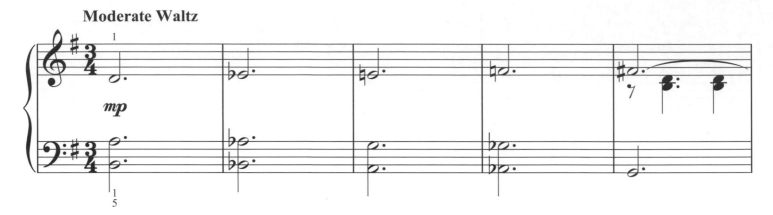

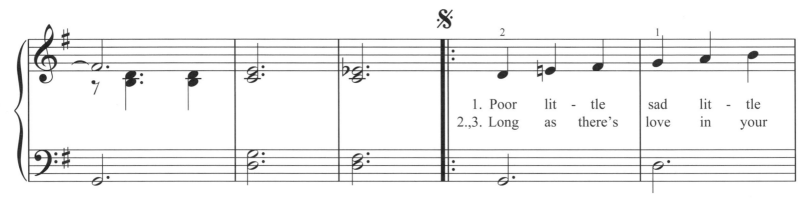

1. Poor lit - tle sad lit - tle
2.,3. Long as there's love in your

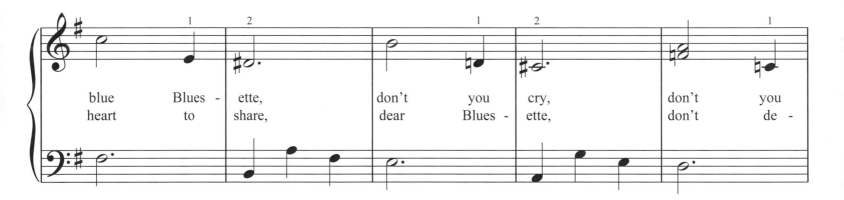

blue Blues - ette, don't you cry, don't you
heart Blues to share, dear Blues - ette, don't de -

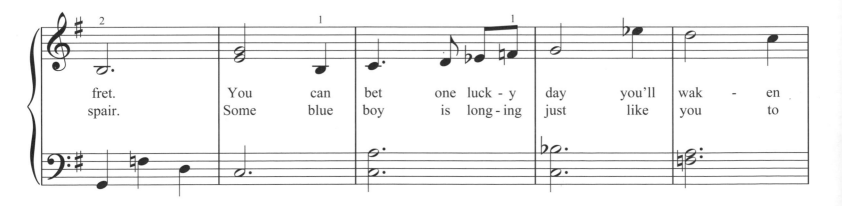

fret. You can bet one luck - y day you'll wak - en
spair. Some blue boy is long - ing just like you to

and your blues will be for - sak - en. (1.,3.) One luck - y
find a some - one to be true to. Two lov - ing

To Coda ⊕ | 1.

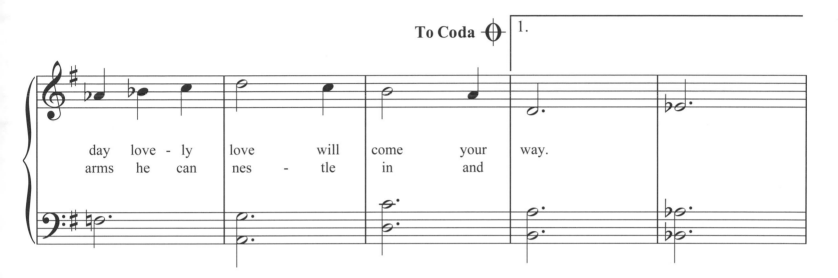

day love - ly love will come your way.
arms he can nes - tle in your and

| 2.

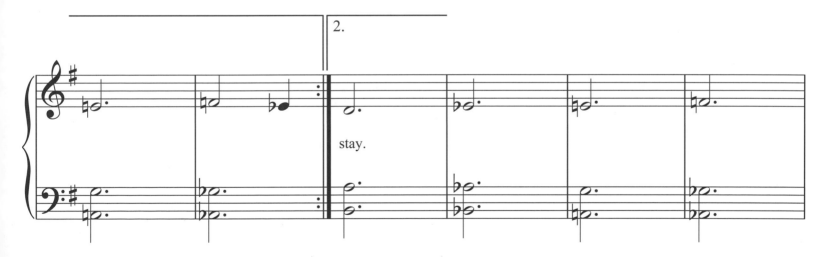

stay.

Get set, Blues - ette, true love is com - ing. Your trou - bled

32

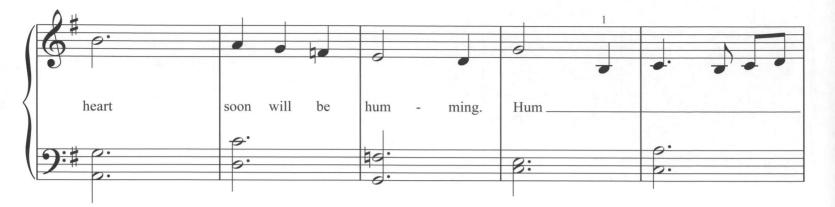

heart   soon will be   hum - ming. Hum _____

_____   Doo - ya, doo - ya, doo - ya,   doo - ya, doo - ya, doo - ya,   doo -   oo -

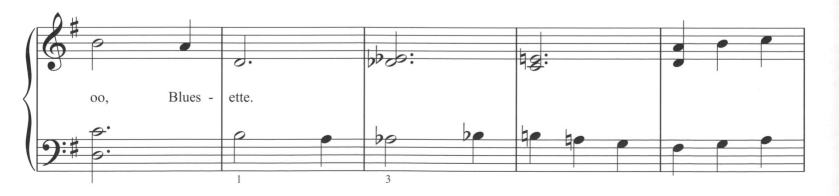

oo,   Blues - ette.

Pret - ty lit - tle Blues - ette, must - n't be a mourn - er.

Have you heard the news yet? Love is 'round the cor - ner. Love wrapped in

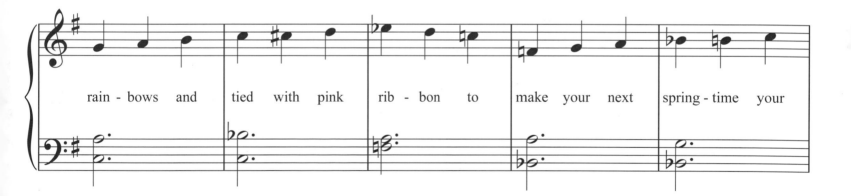

rain - bows and tied with pink rib - bon to make your next spring - time your

gold wed - ding ring time. So, dry your ___ eyes. Don't - cha pout, don't - cha fret,   good - y   good   times   are   com - ing,   Blues - ette._____

CODA

way._____   That   mag - ic

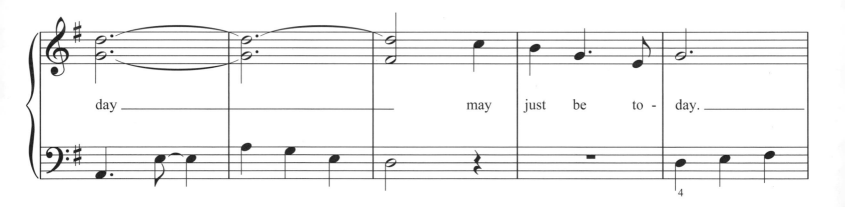

day_____   may   just   be   to - day._____

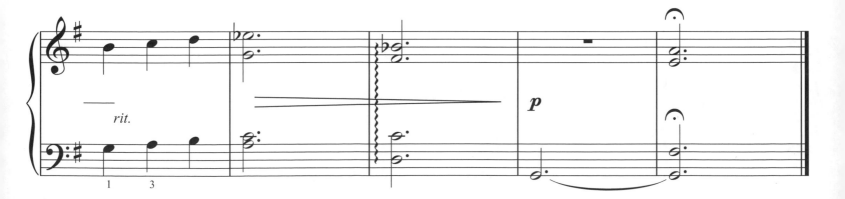

_____ *rit.*   *p*

BUT BEAUTIFUL

from ROAD TO RIO

Words by JOHNNY BURKE
Music by JIMMY VAN HEUSEN

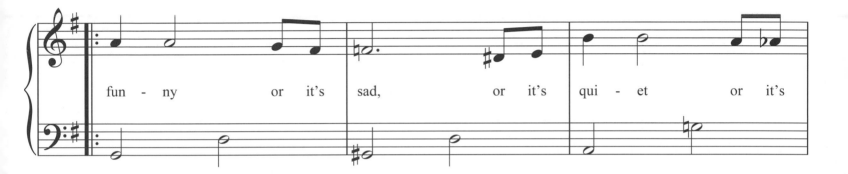

take a chance and if you fall, you fall; and I'm

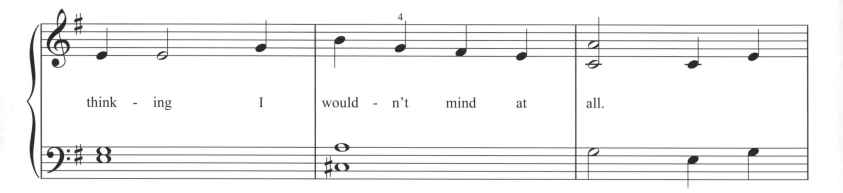

think - ing I would - n't mind at all.

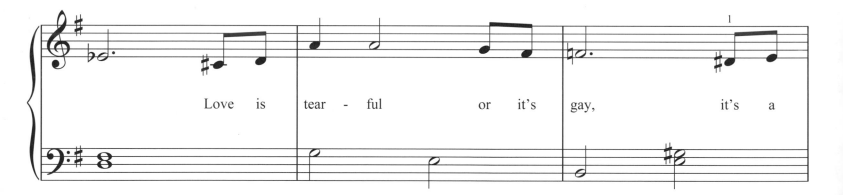

Love is tear - ful or it's gay, it's a

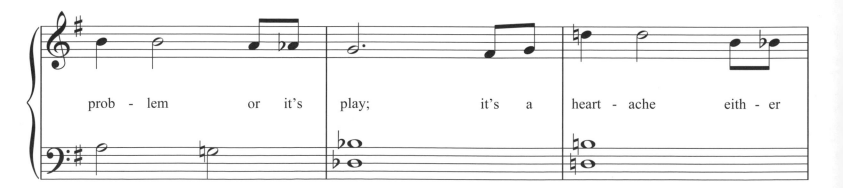

prob - lem or it's play; it's a heart - ache eith - er

way, but beau - ti - ful! _____ And I'm

think - ing if you were mine I'd nev - er let you

go; and that would be but beau - ti - ful I

know. Love is know. know.

CHEEK TO CHEEK
from the RKO Radio Motion Picture TOP HAT

Words and Music by
IRVING BERLIN

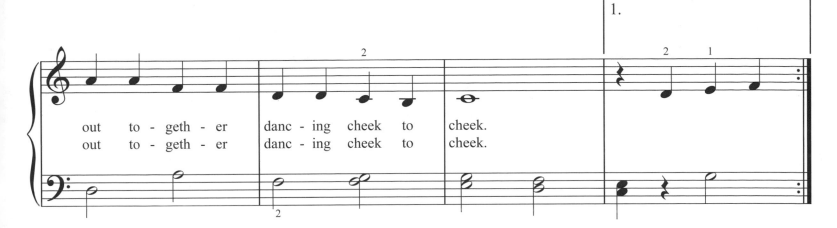

out   to - geth - er   danc - ing   cheek   to   cheek.
out   to - geth - er   danc - ing   cheek   to   cheek.

Oh!   I   love   to   climb   a   moun - tain,   and   to   reach   the   high - est

peak,   but   it   does - n't   thrill   me   half   as   much   as   danc - ing   cheek   to

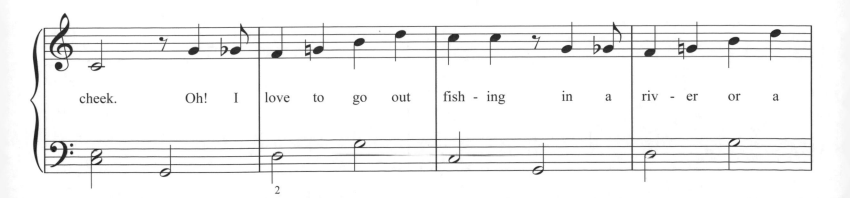

cheek.   Oh!   I   love   to   go   out   fish - ing   in   a   riv - er   or   a

creek, but I don't en - joy it half as much as danc - ing cheek to

cheek. Dance with me ___ I want my arm a - bout you. ___

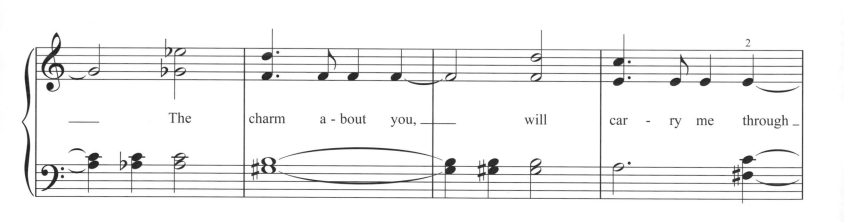

___ The charm a - bout you, ___ will car - ry me through ___

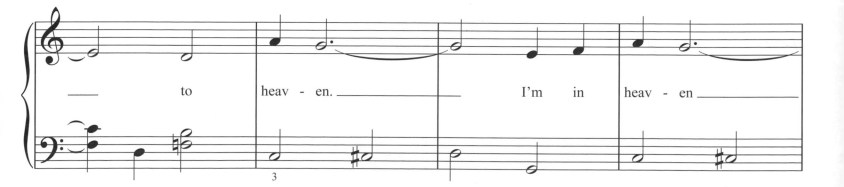

___ to heav - en. ___ I'm in heav - en ___

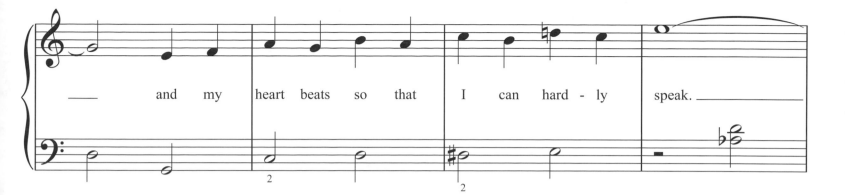

_____ and my heart beats so that I can hard - ly speak. _____

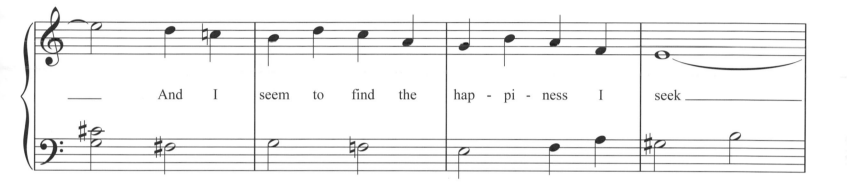

_____ And I seem to find the hap - pi - ness I seek _____

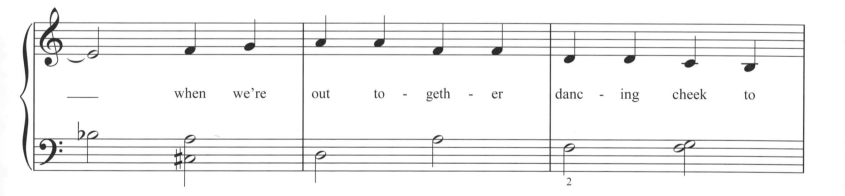

_____ when we're out to - geth - er danc - ing cheek to

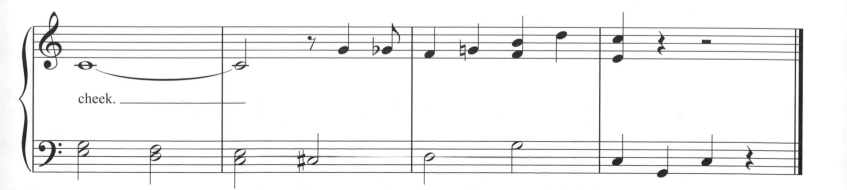

cheek. _____

GENTLE RAIN
from the Motion Picture THE GENTLE RAIN

Music by LUIZ BONFA
Words by MATT DUBEY

Bossa Nova

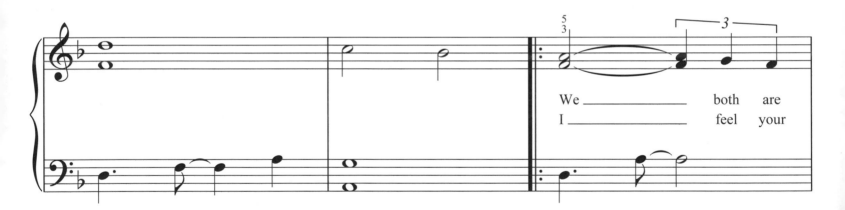

We _____ both are
I _____ feel your

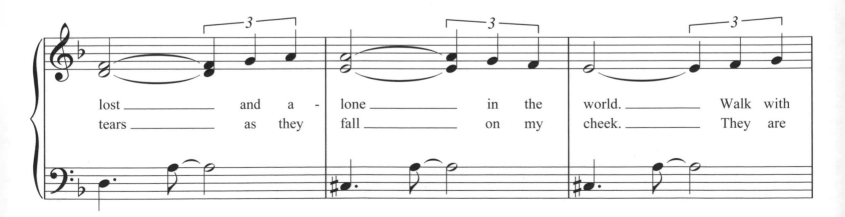

lost _____ and a - lone _____ in the world. _____ Walk with
tears _____ as they fall _____ on my cheek. _____ They are

sad, _____ ver - y sweet, like the gen - tle rain,

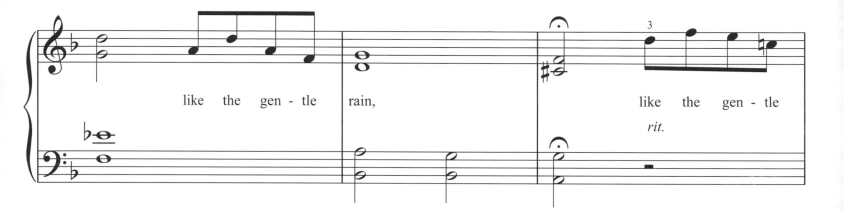

like the gen - tle rain, like the gen - tle

rit.

rain.

a tempo

Like the gen - tle rain. *freely*

COME RAIN OR COME SHINE

from ST. LOUIS WOMAN

Words by JOHNNY MERCER
Music by HAROLD ARLEN

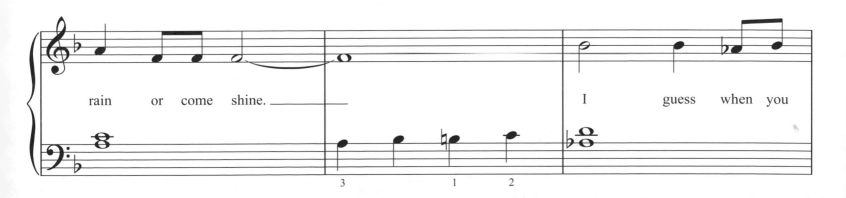

met me it was just one of those things;

but don't ev - er bet me, 'cause I'm gon - na be true if you

let me. You're gon - na love me like no - bod - y's loved me come

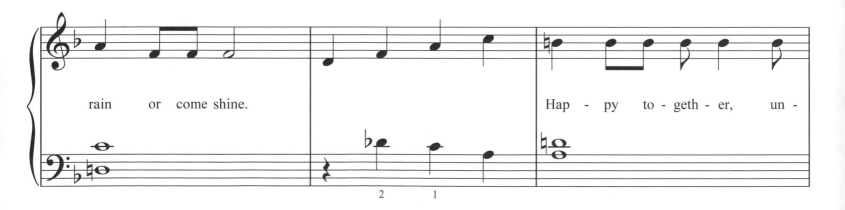

rain or come shine. Hap - py to - geth - er, un -

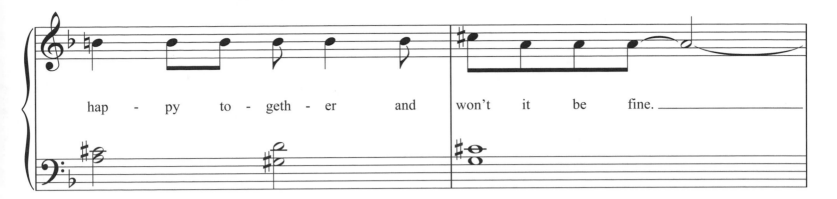

hap - py to - geth - er and won't it be fine. _____

_____ Days may be cloud - y or sun - ny, we're

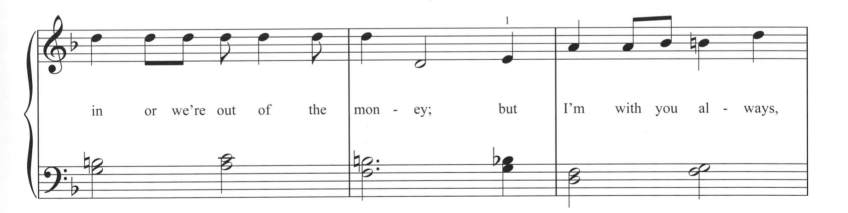

in or we're out of the mon - ey; but I'm with you al - ways,

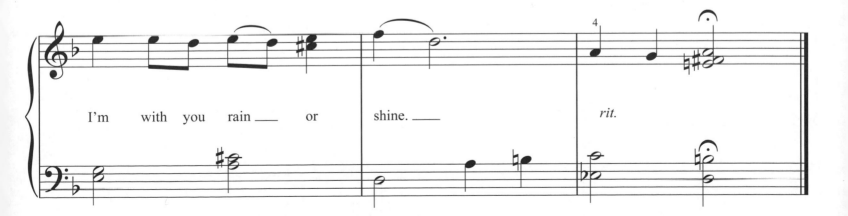

I'm with you rain ___ or shine. ___

rit.

EMBRACEABLE YOU
from GIRL CRAZY

Music and Lyrics by GEORGE GERSHWIN
and IRA GERSHWIN

Whimsically

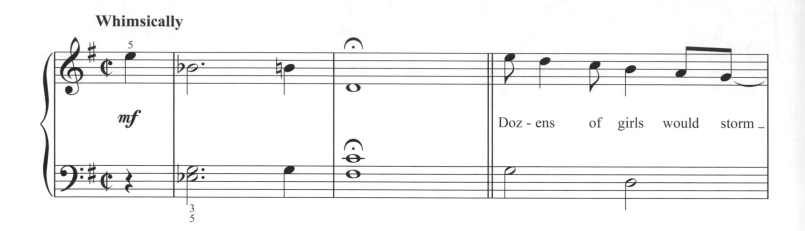

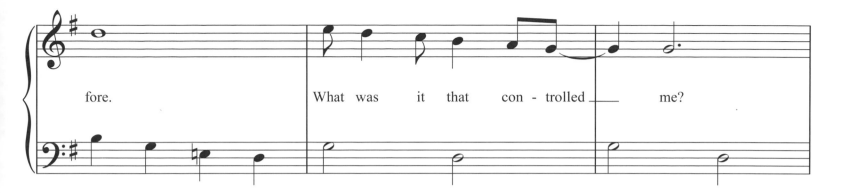

fore. What was it that con - trolled ____ me?

What kept my love - life lean? My in - tu - i - tion told _

__ me you'd come on the scene. La- dy, lis - ten to the rhy - thm of my

heart - beat, and you'll get just what I mean.

Em - brace me, my sweet em - brace - a - ble you!

Em - brace me, you ir - re - place - a - ble you!

Just one look at you, my heart grew tip - sy in me;

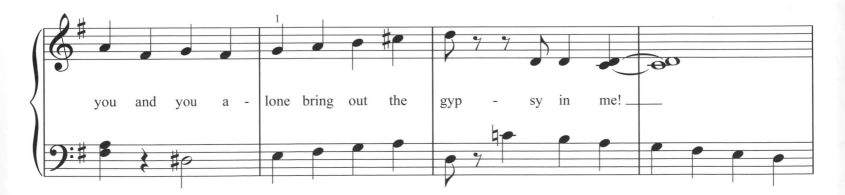

you and you a - lone bring out the gyp - sy in me!

I love all the man - y charms a - bout you;

a - bove all, I want my arms a - bout you.

Don't be a naugh - ty ba - by, Come to pa - pa, come to pa - pa, do!

My sweet em - brace - a - ble you!

EMILY

from the MGM Motion Picture THE AMERICANIZATION OF EMILY

Music by JOHNNY MANDEL
Words by JOHNNY MERCER

Moderately slow, with freedom

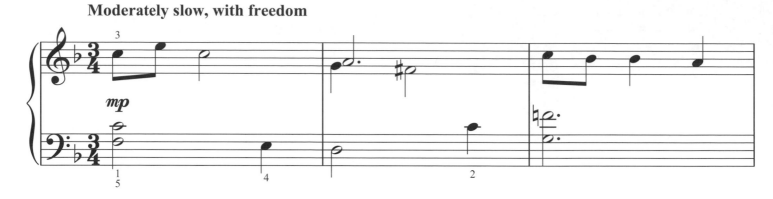

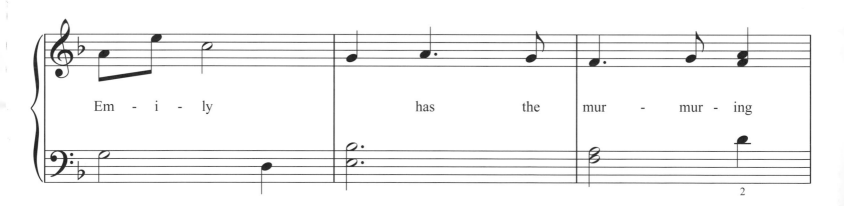

silver bells, coral shells, carousels,

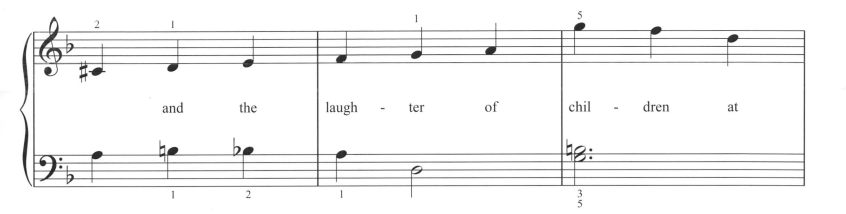

and the laughter of children at

play say: Emily,

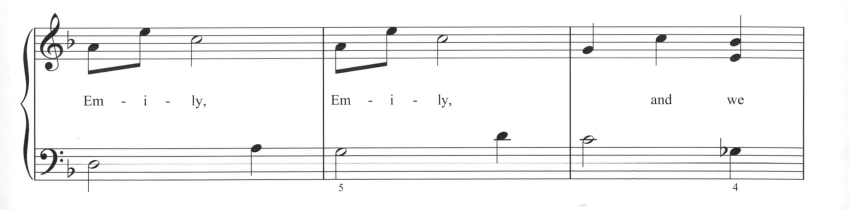

Emily, Emily, and we

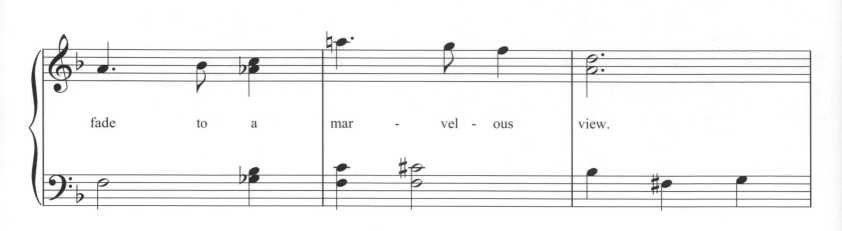

fade   to   a   mar - vel - ous   view.

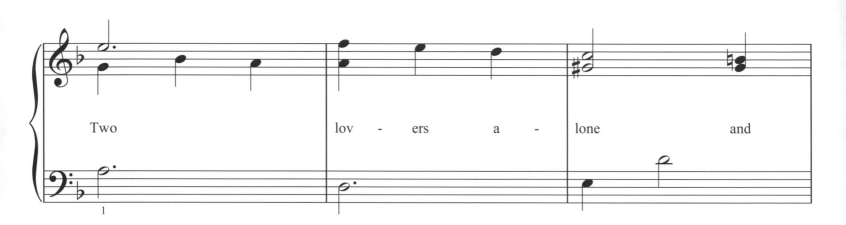

Two   lov - ers   a - lone   and

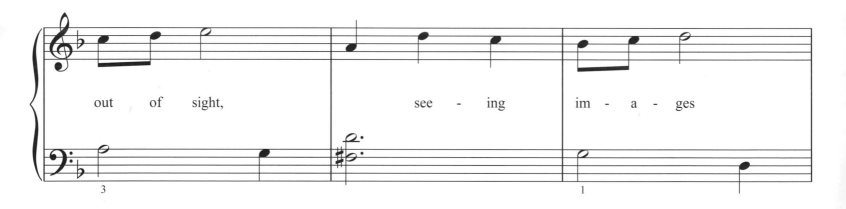

out   of   sight,   see - ing   im - a - ges

in   the   fire - light.   As   my

eyes   vis - ual - ize   a   fam - i - ly, _____

_____   they   see   dream - i - ly,   Em - i - ly,

too.   too.

HERE'S THAT RAINY DAY
from CARNIVAL IN FLANDERS

Words by JOHNNY BURKE
Music by JIMMY VAN HEUSEN

Very slowly

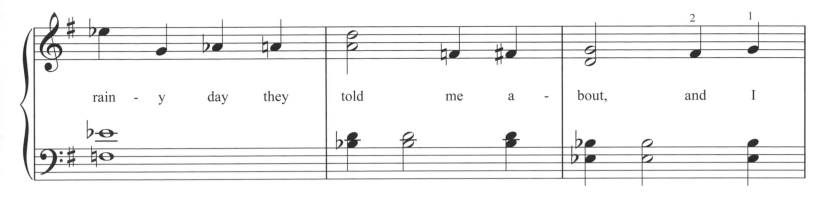

rain - y day they told me a - bout, and I

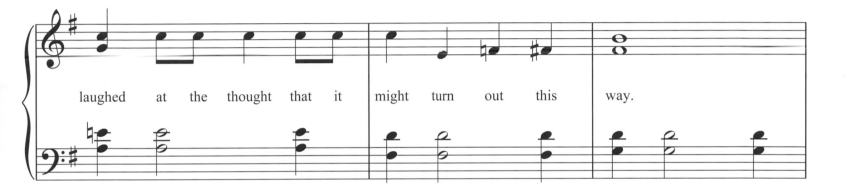

laughed at the thought that it might turn out this way.

Where is that worn - out wish that

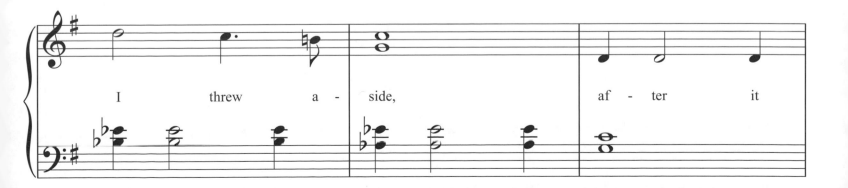

I threw a - side, af - ter it

brought my lov - er near? _____

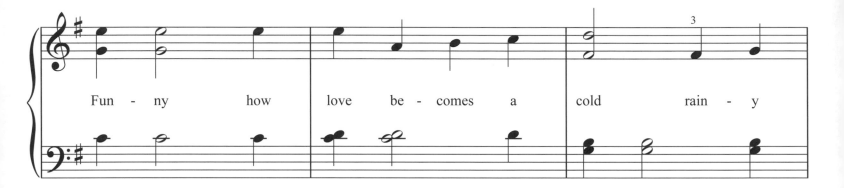

Fun - ny how love be - comes a cold rain - y

day. Fun - ny, that rain - y day is

1. here.

2. here.

I GET A KICK OUT OF YOU

from ANYTHING GOES

Words and Music by
COLE PORTER

Moderately

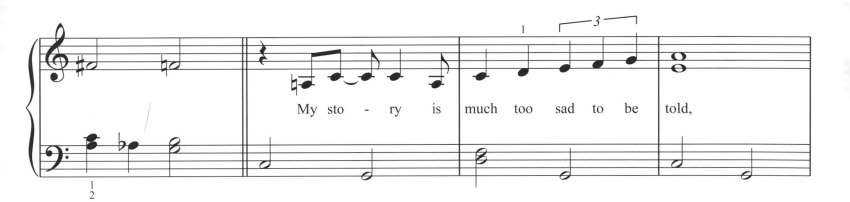

My sto - ry is much too sad to be told,

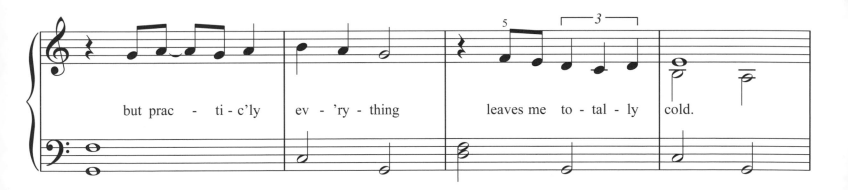

but prac - ti - c'ly ev - 'ry - thing leaves me to - tal - ly cold.

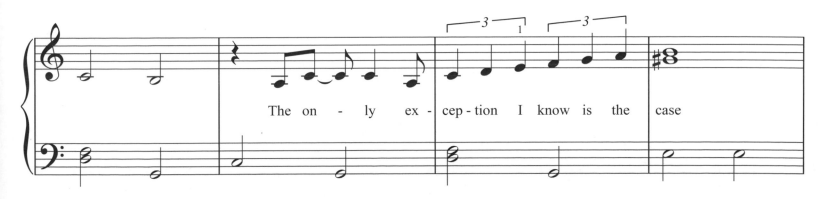

The on - ly ex - cep - tion I know is the case

where I'm out on a quiet spree, _ fight-ing vain-ly the old en-nui, _

and I sud-den-ly turn and see __ your fab-u-lous face.

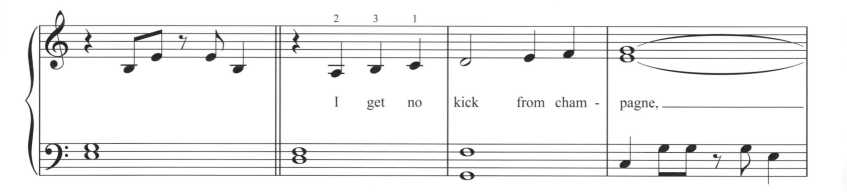

I get no kick from cham - pagne, ___

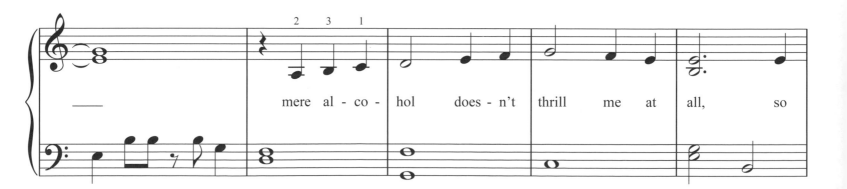

__ mere al-co-hol does-n't thrill me at all, so

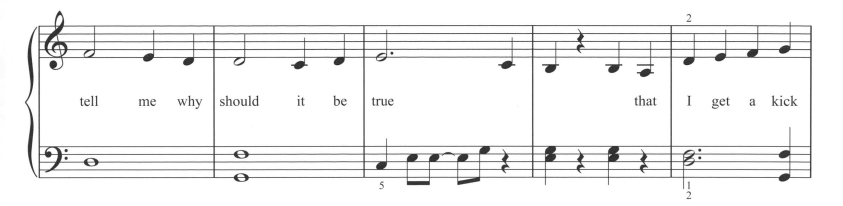

tell me why should it be true that I get a kick

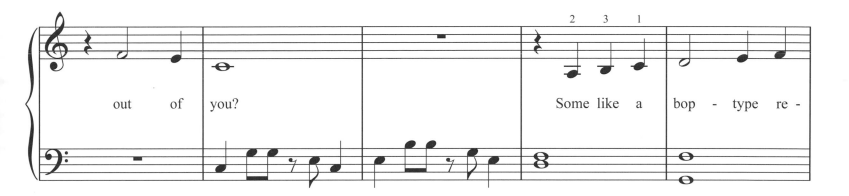

out of you? Some like a bop - type re -

frain; I'm sure that if I heard e - ven one

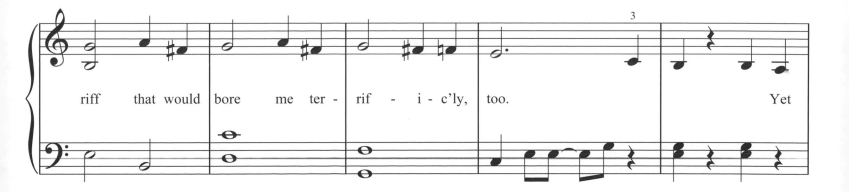

riff that would bore me ter - rif - i - c'ly, too. Yet

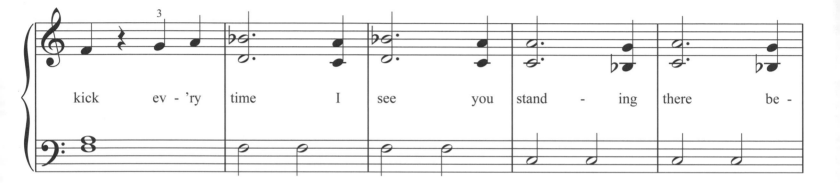

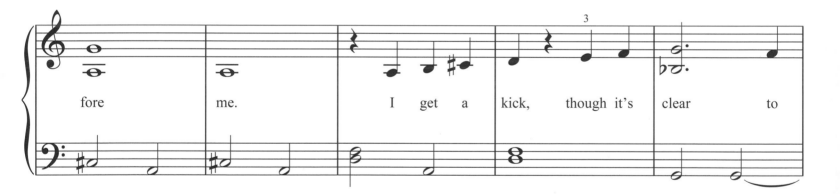

63

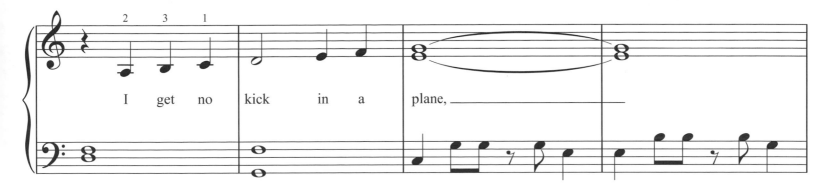

I get no kick in a plane, ____

fly - ing too high with some guy in the sky is my i - dea of

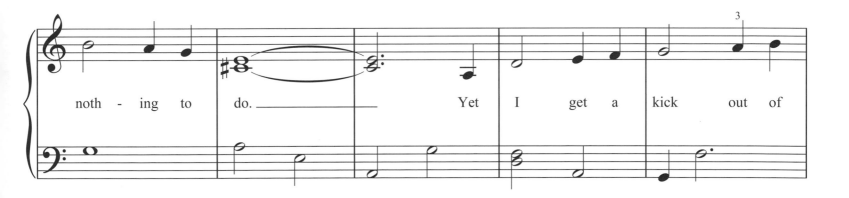

noth - ing to do. ____ Yet I get a kick out of

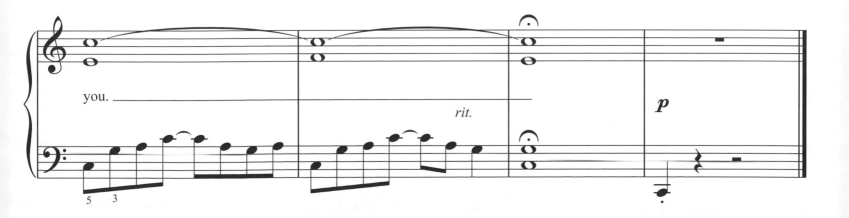

you. ____ *rit.* *p*

I'VE GOT YOU UNDER MY SKIN

from BORN TO DANCE

Words and Music by
COLE PORTER

Moderate Beguine feel

heart of me, _____ so deep in my heart _____

_____ you're real - ly a part of me. _____ I've

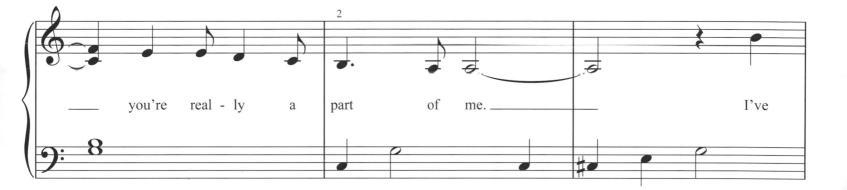

got you un - der my skin. I

tried so _____ not to give in. I

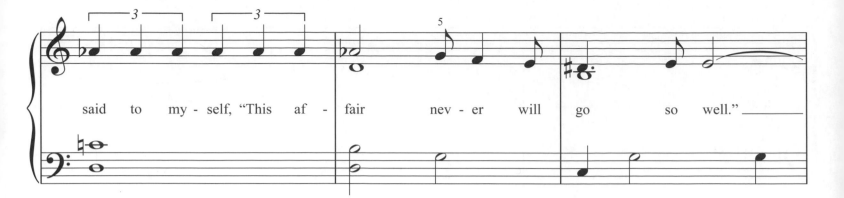

said to my-self, "This af - fair nev-er will go so well." ____

____ But why should I try to re - sist when, dar - ling, I

know so well? I've got you ____

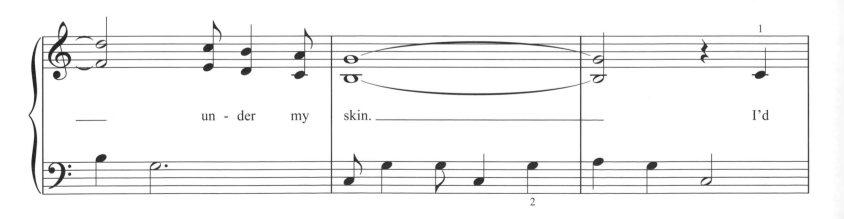

____ un - der my skin. ____ I'd

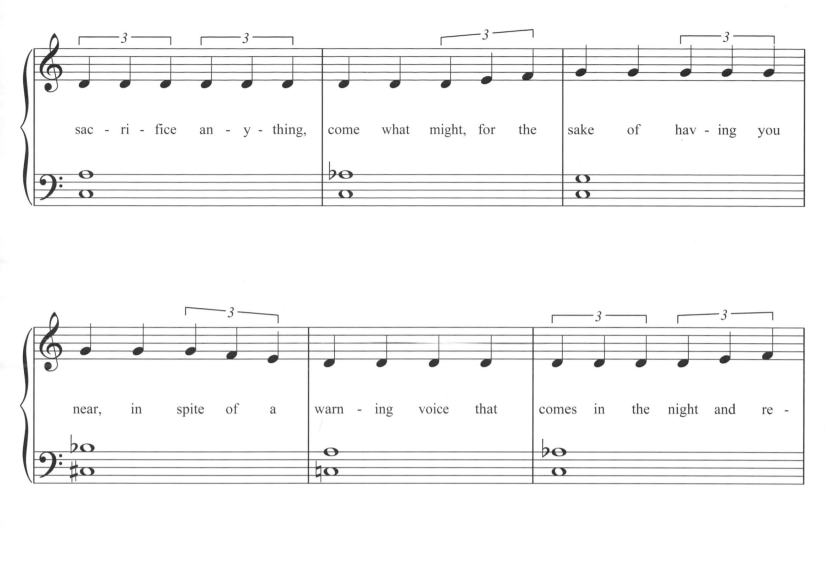

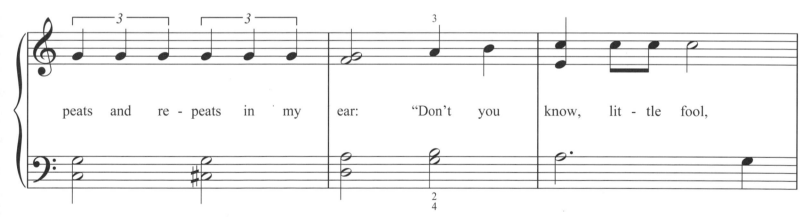

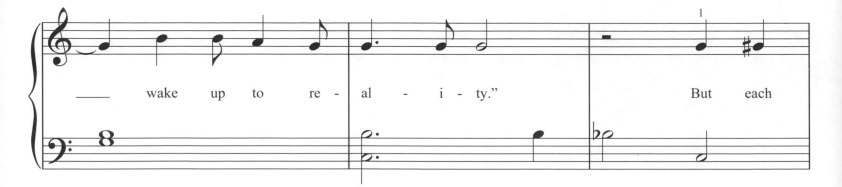

_____ wake up to re - al - i - ty." But each

time I do, just the thought of you makes me stop be - fore I be -

gin, 'cause I've got you _____ un - der my

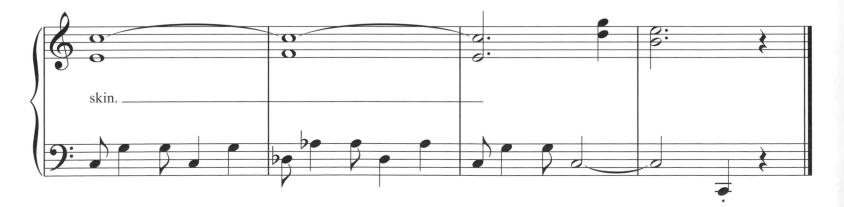

skin. _____

ISN'T IT ROMANTIC?
from the Paramount Picture LOVE ME TONIGHT

Words by LORENZ HART
Music by RICHARD RODGERS

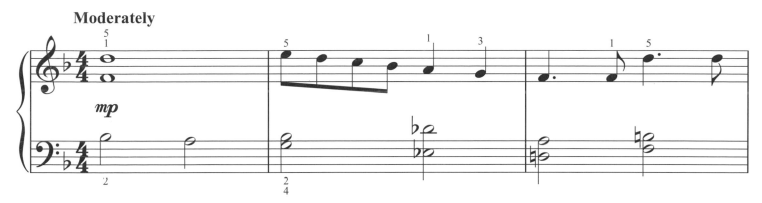

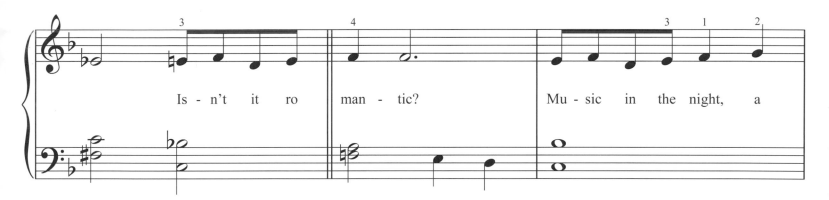

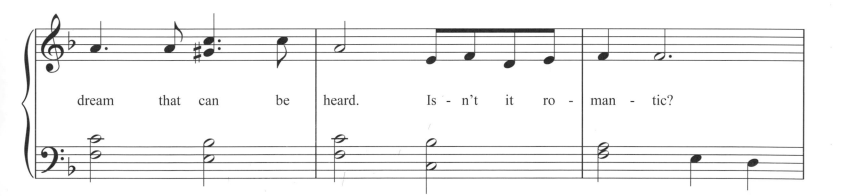

70

I hear the breez - es play - ing in the trees a -

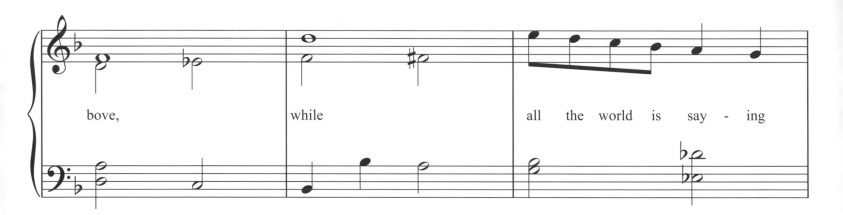

bove, while all the world is say - ing

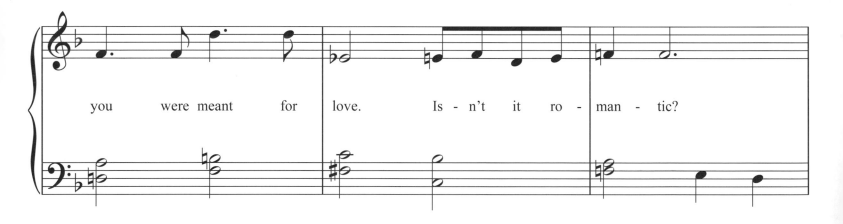

you were meant for love. Is - n't it ro - man - tic?

Mere - ly to be young on such a night as this? Is - n't it ro -

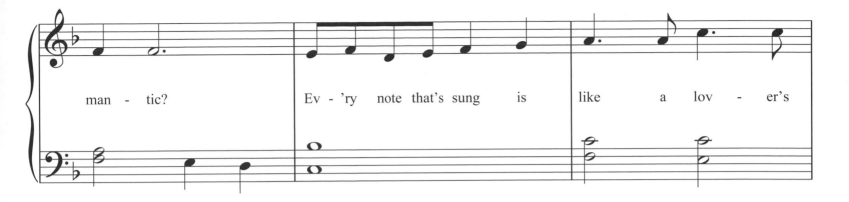

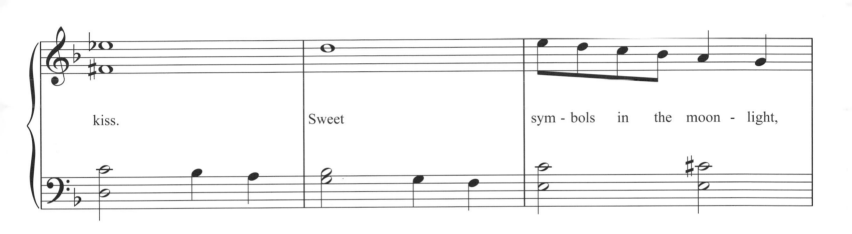

IF YOU COULD SEE ME NOW

Lyric by CARL SIGMAN
Music by TADD DAMERON

Moderately

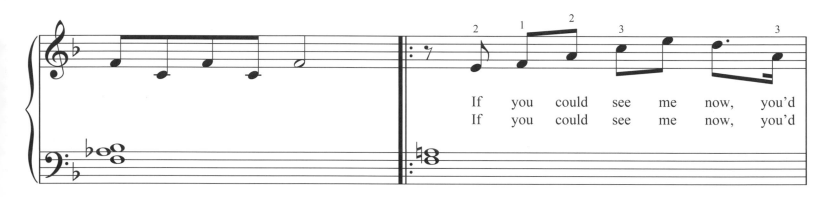

If you could see me now, you'd
If you could see me now, you'd

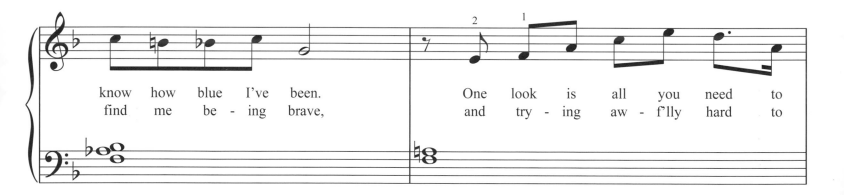

know how blue I've been.
find me be - ing brave,

One look is all you need to
and try - ing aw - f'lly hard to

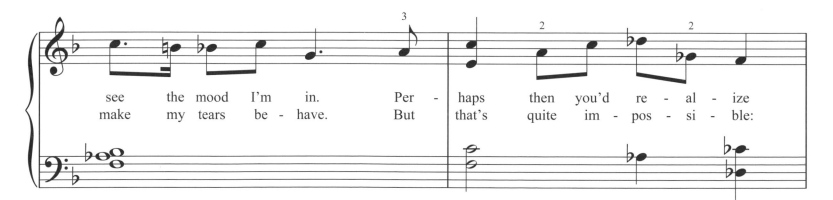

see the mood I'm in. Per -
make my tears be - have. But

haps then you'd re - al - ize
that's quite im - pos - si - ble:

I'm _____ still in love _____ with you.
I'm _____ still in love _____ with

you.

Slow Swing

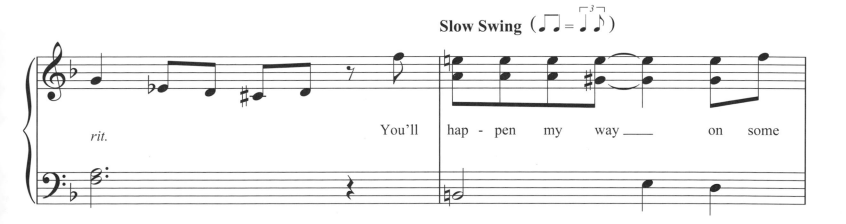

rit.

You'll hap - pen my way _____ on some

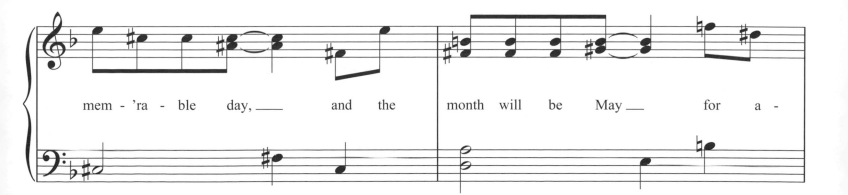

mem - 'ra - ble day, _____ and the   month will be May _____ for a -

74

while.   I'll   try   to   smile, —   but   can - not   play   the

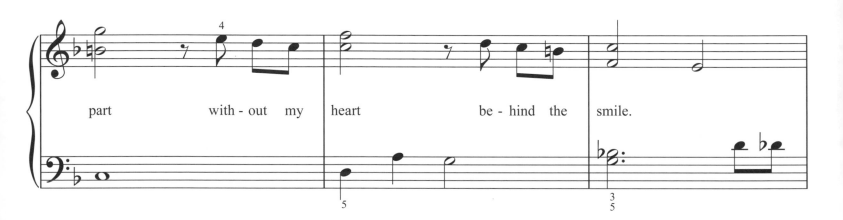

part   with - out   my   heart   be - hind   the   smile.

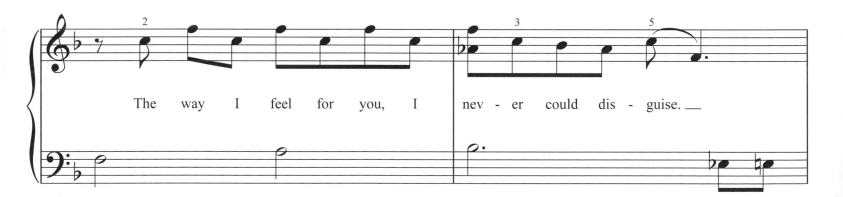

The   way   I   feel   for   you,   I   nev - er   could   dis - guise. —

The   look   of   love   is   writ - ten   plain - ly   in   your   eyes. —

I think you'd be mine a - gain   if you could see me

now.

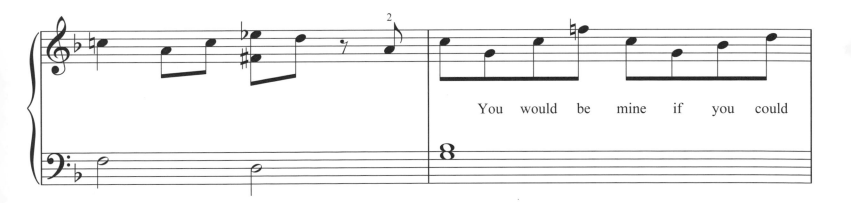

You would be mine if you could

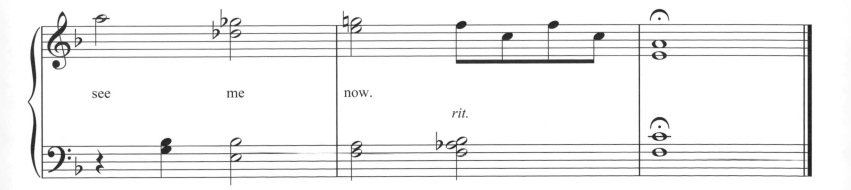

see   me   now.

rit.

IN YOUR OWN SWEET WAY

By DAVE BRUBECK

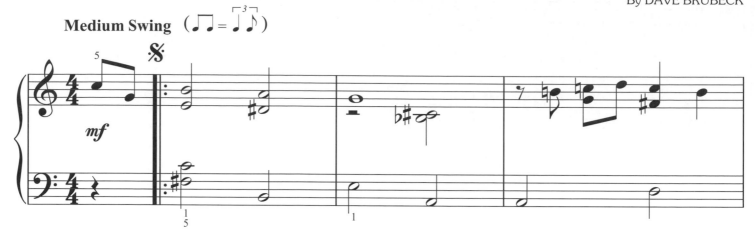

D.S. al Coda

CODA

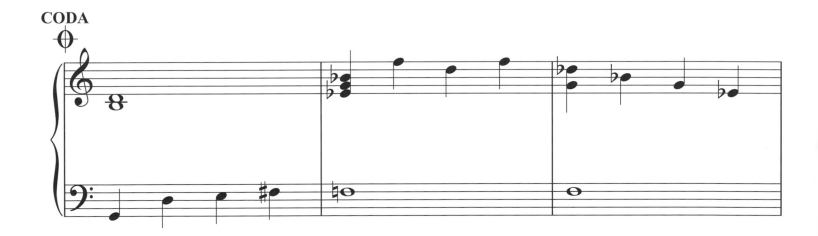

rit.

IT HAD TO BE YOU

Words by GUS KAHN
Music by ISHAM JONES

Moderate Swing

Why do I do just as you say? __ Why must I just
Seems like dreams do like I al - ways had __ could be, should be,

give you your way? __ Why do I sigh? __
mak - ing me glad. __ Why am I blue? __

79

Why don't I try __ to for - get?
It's up to you __ to ex - plain.

It must have
I'm think - ing

been that some - thing
may - be, ba - by,

lov - ers call fate; __
I'll go a - way. __

kept on say - ing
Some day, some way,

I had to wait. __
you'll come and say, __

I saw it all, __
"It's you I need," __

just could - n't fall __ till we
and you'll be plead - ing in

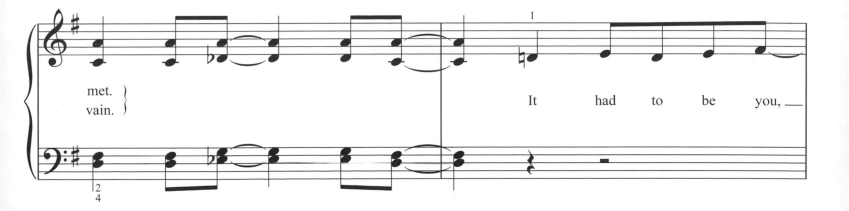

met.
vain.

It had to be you, __

it had to be you. ___ I wan-dered a - round ___

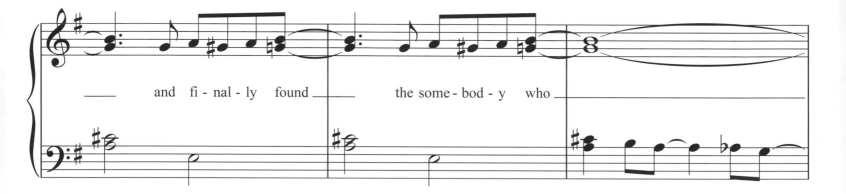

___ and fi - nal - ly found ___ the some - bod - y who ___

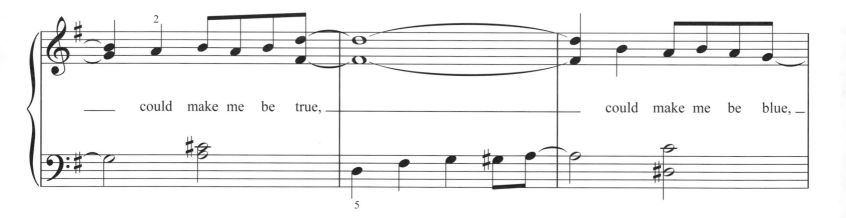

___ could make me be true, ___ could make me be blue, __

___ and e - ven be glad, ___ just to be sad, __

think - ing of you. _____ Some oth - ers I've seen _

might nev - er be mean, _____

might nev - er be cross _____ or try to be boss, _____ but they would - n't do. _

For no - bod - y else _____ gave me a thrill. _

With all your faults, ___ I love you still. ___ It had to be you, ___

To Coda ⊕ | 1.

___ won - der - ful you, ___ had to be you. ___

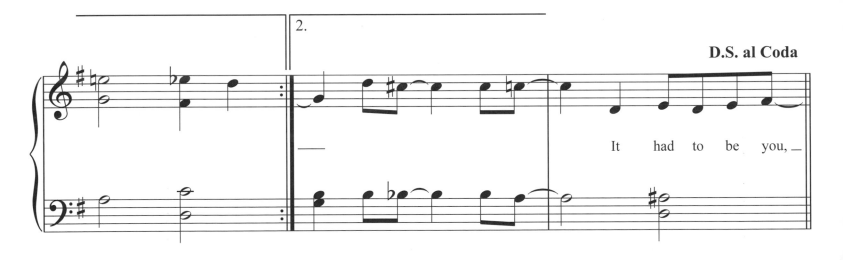

2.   D.S. al Coda

___ It had to be you, ___

CODA

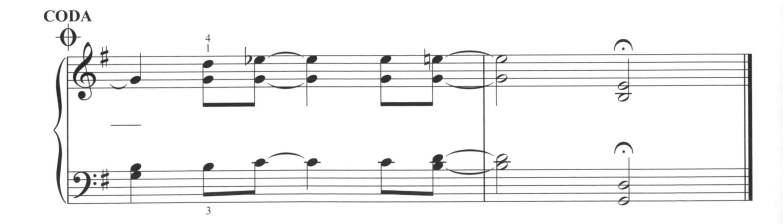

THE LAMP IS LOW

Music by PETER DeROSE and BERT SHEFTER
Words by MITCHELL PARISH
Original French Lyrics by YVETTE BARUCH
Melody based on a Theme from Ravel's PAVANE

Slowly, with much expression

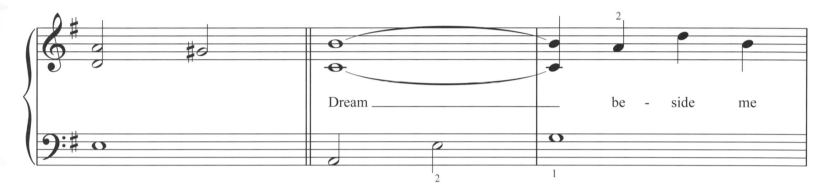

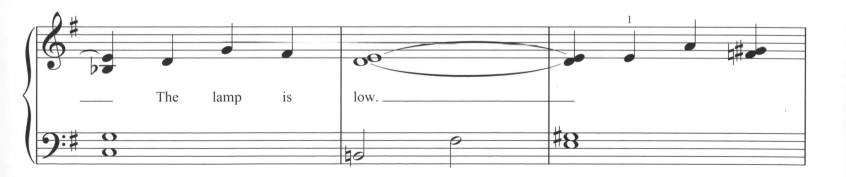

84

Dream, _____ and watch the shad - ows come and

go. _____ The lamp is low.

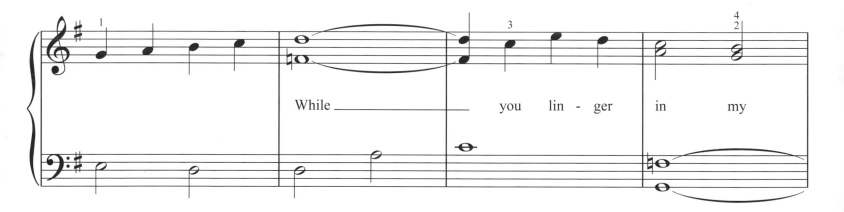

While _____ you lin - ger in my

arms, my lips will sigh, _____ "I love you

so." _____ Dream _____

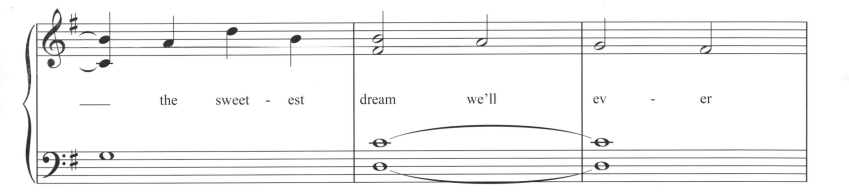

_____ the sweet - est dream we'll ev - er

know. _____ To - night the moon is high,

the lamp is low. _____
rit.

LIKE SOMEONE IN LOVE

Words by JOHNNY BURKE
Music by JIMMY VAN HEUSEN

Slowly, with expression

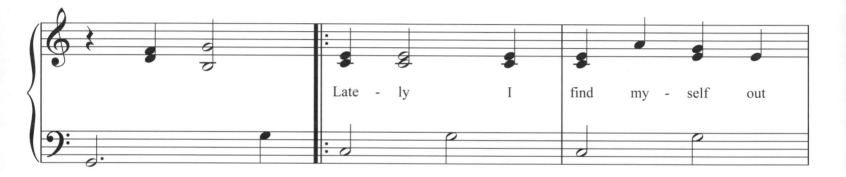

Some - times the things I do a - stound me, ____

____ most - ly when - ev - er you're a -

round me. Late - ly I seem to walk as

though I had wings, bump in - to

things   like   some - one   in   love.

Each   time   I   look   at   you,   I'm   limp   as   a

glove   and   feel - ing   like   some - one   in

1.   love.   2.   love.

LITTLE SUNFLOWER

By FREDDIE HUBBARD

Medium Latin

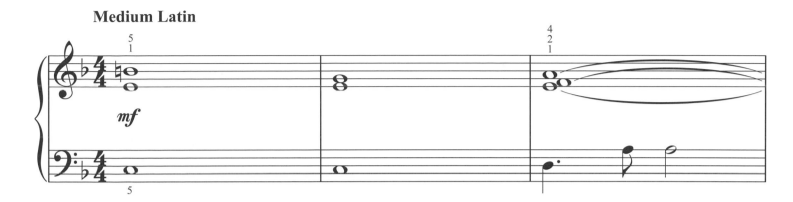

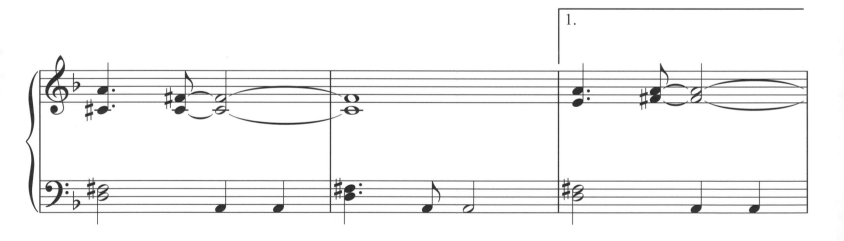

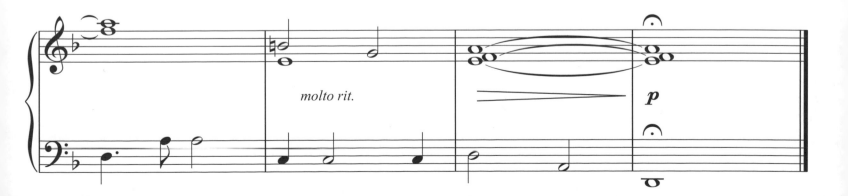

molto rit.

p

LOVE FOR SALE
from THE NEW YORKERS

Words and Music by
COLE PORTER

Lively Latin feel

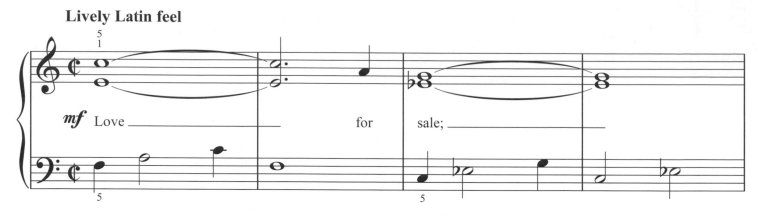

Love _____ for sale;

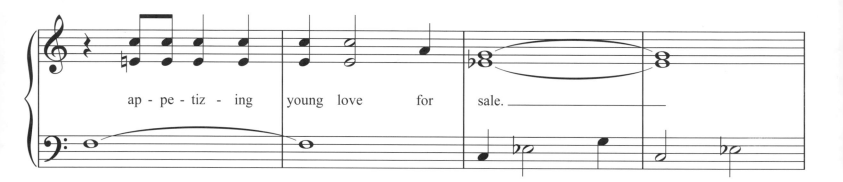

ap - pe - tiz - ing young love for sale. _____

Love that's fresh and still un - spoiled, love that's on - ly

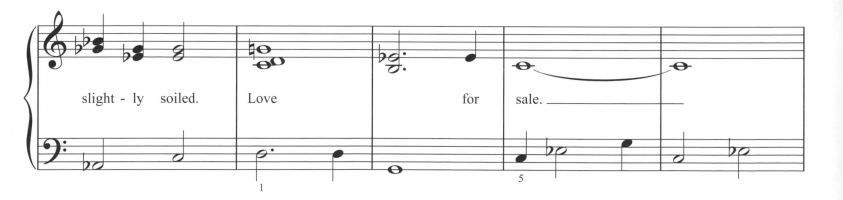

slight - ly soiled. Love for sale. _____

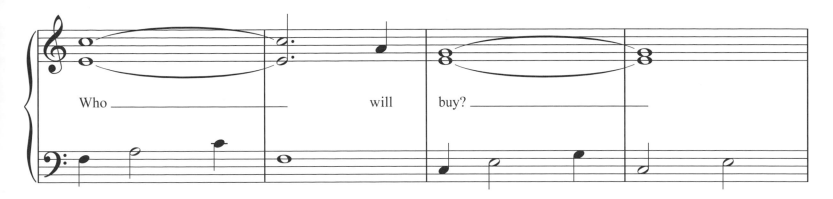

Who _____ will buy? _____

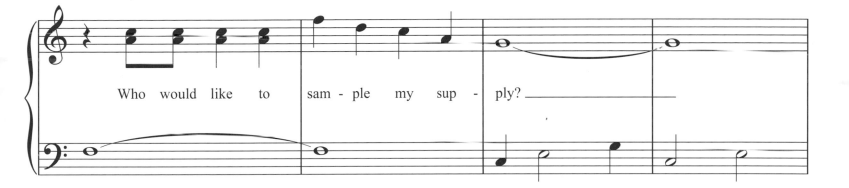

Who would like to sam - ple my sup - ply? _____

Who's pre - pared to pay the price for a trip to

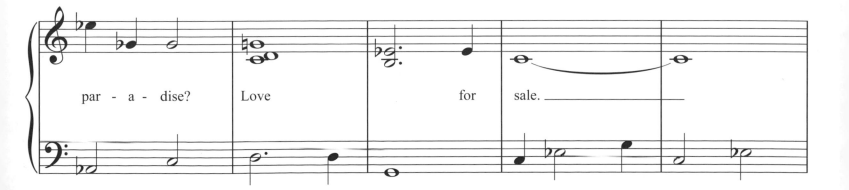

par - a - dise? Love for sale. _____

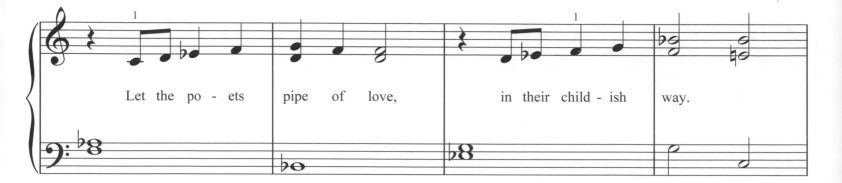

Let the po - ets pipe of love, in their child - ish way.

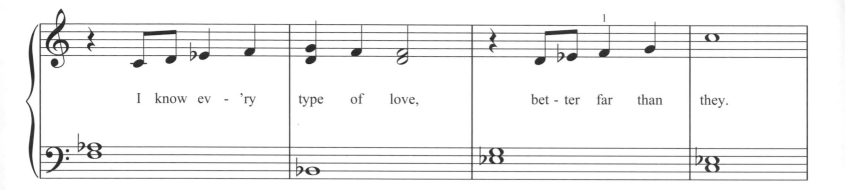

I know ev - 'ry type of love, bet - ter far than they.

If you want the thrill of love, I've been through the mill of love;

old love, new love, ev - 'ry love, but true love.

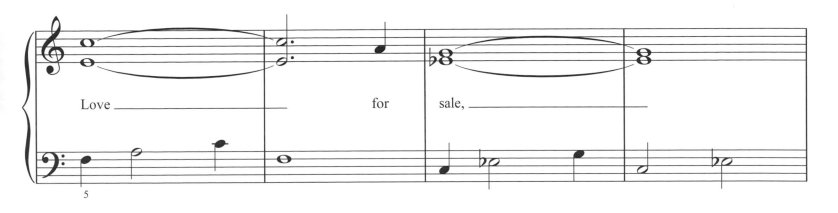

Love _____ for sale, _____

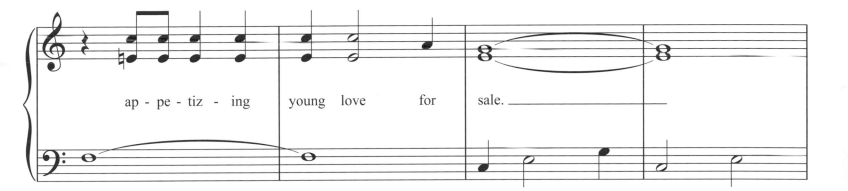

ap - pe - tiz - ing young love for sale. _____

If you want to buy my wares, fol - low me and climb the stairs.

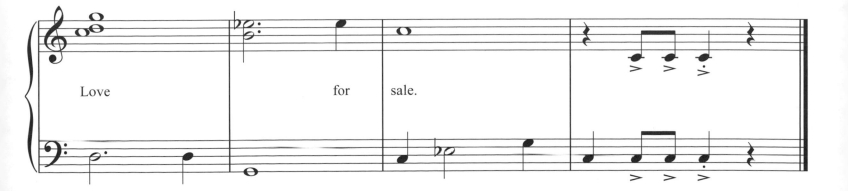

Love for sale.

LOVE IS HERE TO STAY

from GOLDWYN FOLLIES

Music and Lyrics by GEORGE GERSHWIN
and IRA GERSHWIN

With motion

The more I read the pa- pers the less I com- pre-

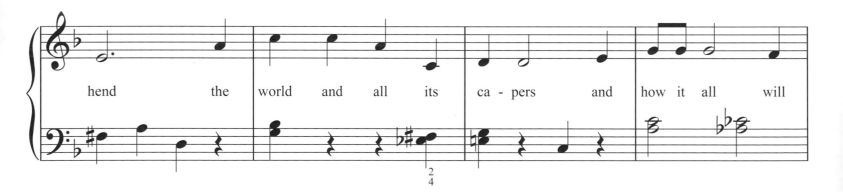

hend the world and all its ca- pers and how it all will

end. Noth- ing seems to be last- ing, but

that is - n't our af - fair; we've got some - thing

per - ma - nent, I mean in the way _____ we

care. _____ It's ver - y clear

our love is here to stay; not for a year

98

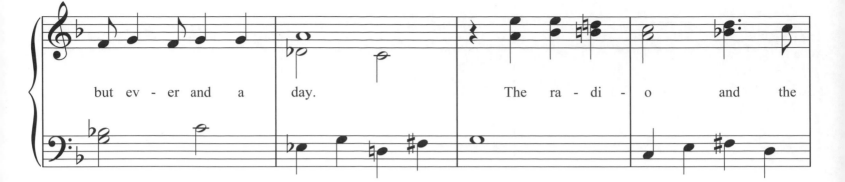

but ev - er and a day. The ra - di - o and the

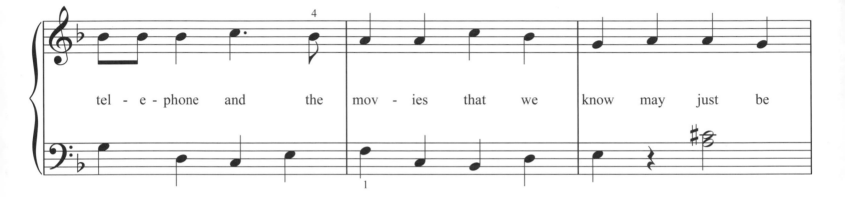

tel - e - phone and the mov - ies that we know may just be

pass - ing fan - cies and in time may go.

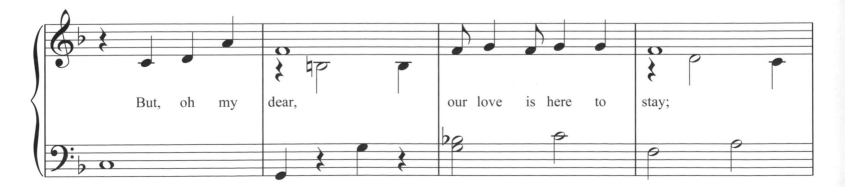

But, oh my dear, our love is here to stay;

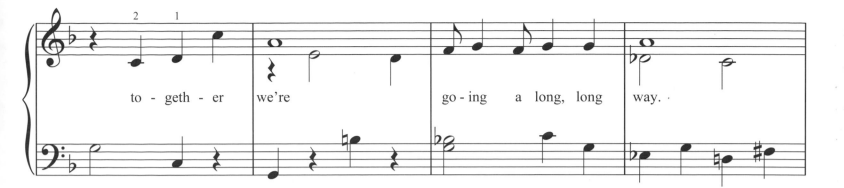

to - geth - er   we're   go - ing   a long, long   way.

In   time   the   Rock - ies may crum - ble,   Gi - bral - tar may   tum - ble,

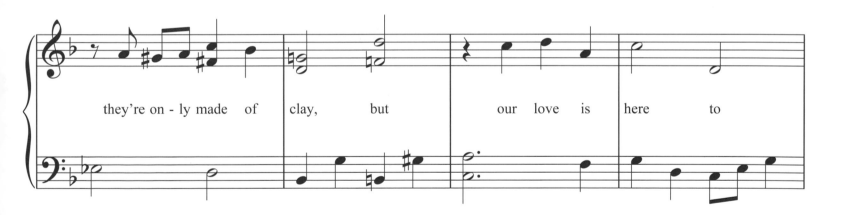

they're on - ly made of   clay,   but   our love is   here   to

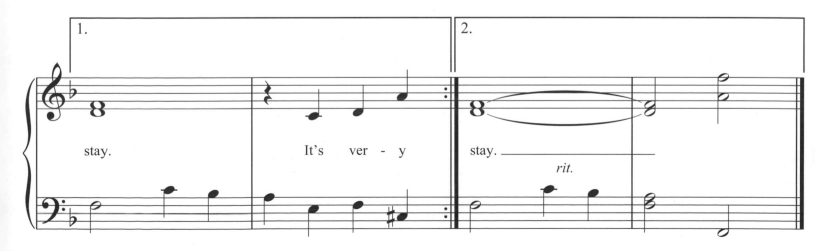

1.   2.

stay.   It's ver - y   stay. _____
                                                        rit.

LULLABY OF BIRDLAND

Words by GEORGE DAVID WEISS
Music by GEORGE SHEARING

Medium Swing

Lull - a - by of Bird - land

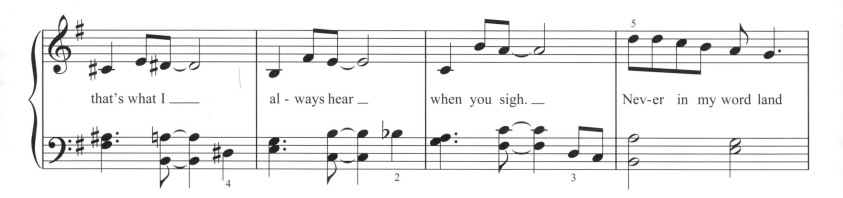

that's what I _____ al - ways hear _____ when you sigh. _____ Nev-er in my word land

could there be ways _____ to re - veal, _____ in a phrase, _____ how I feel! _____

Have you ev - er heard two tur - tle - doves _____ bill and coo _____

when they love? _ That's the kind of mag - ic mu - sic we make _ with our lips _

_____ when we kiss! ___ And there's a weep - y old wil -

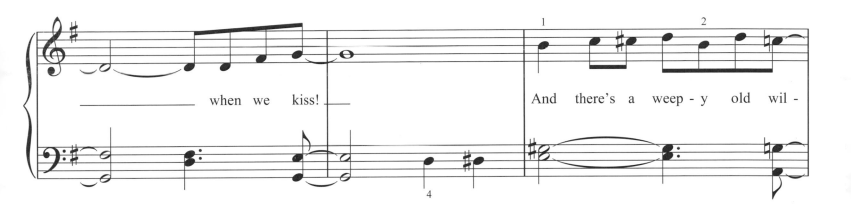

- low, _____ he real - ly knows how to cry. ___

That's how I'd cry in my pil - low _____ if you should tell me fare - well _

102

and good - bye. ___ Lull - a - by of Bird-land whis - per low, ___

kiss me sweet ___ and we'll go ___ fly - in' high in Bird-land

1.

high in the sky ___ up a - bove ___ all be - cause ___ we're in love. ___

2.

___ all be - cause ___ we're in love. ___

THE MORE I SEE YOU

from the Twentieth Century-Fox Technicolor Musical BILLY ROSE'S DIAMOND HORSESHOE

Words by MACK GORDON
Music by HARRY WARREN

Unhurried

The more I see you,

the more I want you. Some - how this

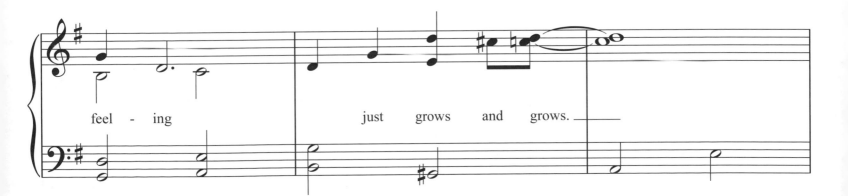

feel - ing just grows and grows.

104

With ev - 'ry sigh I be - come more mad a -

bout you, more lost with - out you, and so it goes.

Can you i - mag - ine

how much I love you? The more I

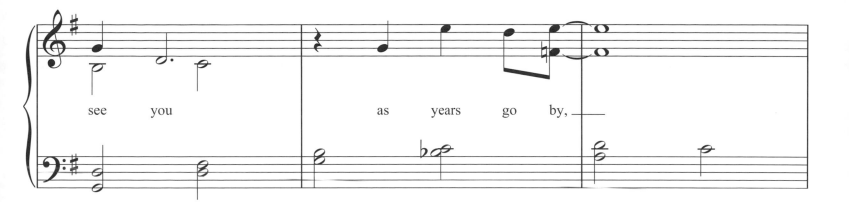

see   you   as   years   go   by,

I   know   the   on - ly   one   for   me   can   on - ly

be   you.   My   arms   won't   free   you,   and   my   heart   won't

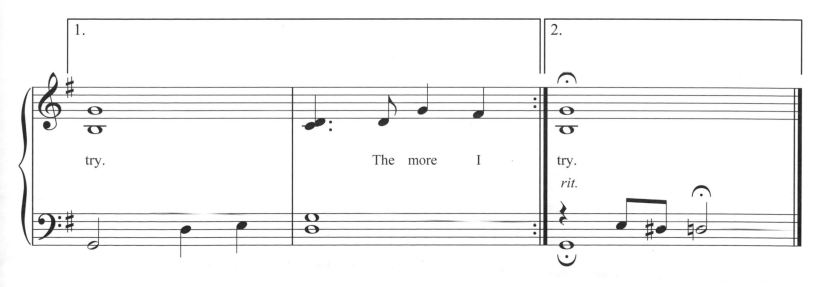

1.

try.   The   more   I   try.

2.

rit.

MACK THE KNIFE
from THE THREEPENNY OPERA

English Words by MARC BLITZSTEIN
Original German Words by BERT BRECHT
Music by KURT WEILL

Moderately

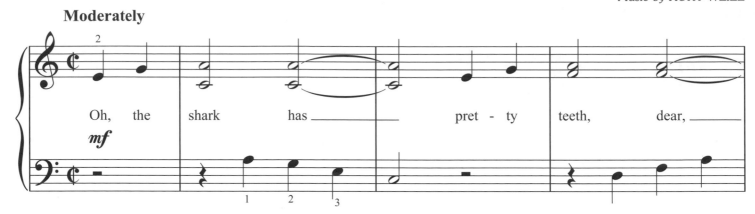

Oh, the shark has _____ pret - ty teeth, dear, _____

mf

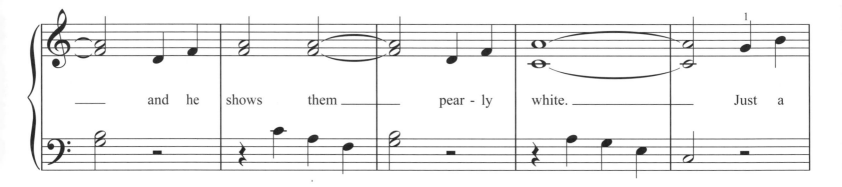

____ and he shows them ____ pear - ly white. ____ Just a

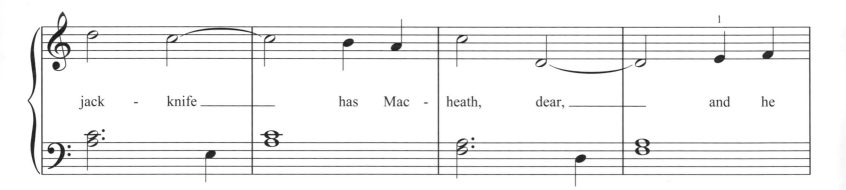

jack - knife _____ has Mac - heath, dear, _____ and he

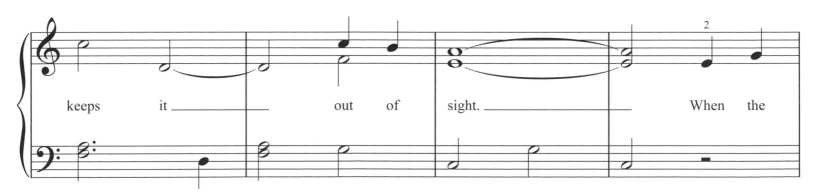

keeps it _____ out of sight. _____ When the

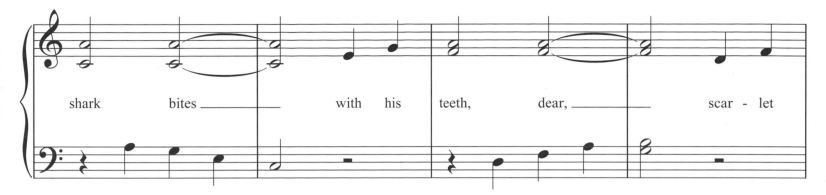

shark   bites _____   with his teeth, dear, _____   scar - let

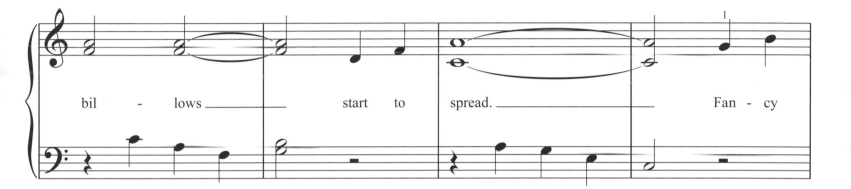

bil - lows _____   start to spread. _____   Fan - cy

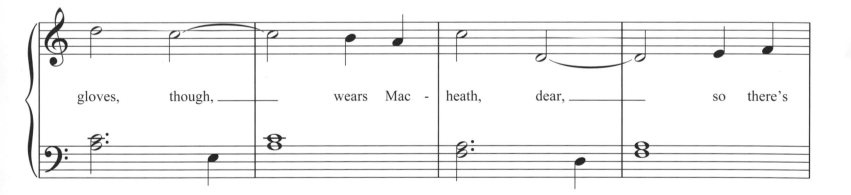

gloves,   though, _____   wears Mac - heath, dear, _____   so there's

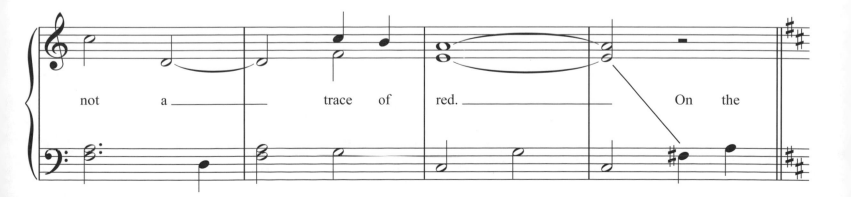

not   a _____   trace of red. _____   On the

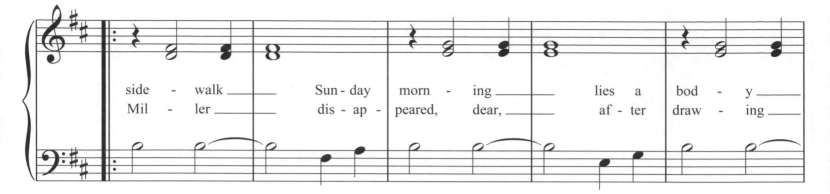

side - walk _____ Sun - day morn - ing _____ lies a bod - y _____
Mil - ler _____ dis - ap - peared, dear, _____ af - ter draw - ing _____

_____ ooz - ing life: _____ some - one's sneak - ing _____ 'round the
_____ out his cash; _____ and Mac - heath spends _____ like a

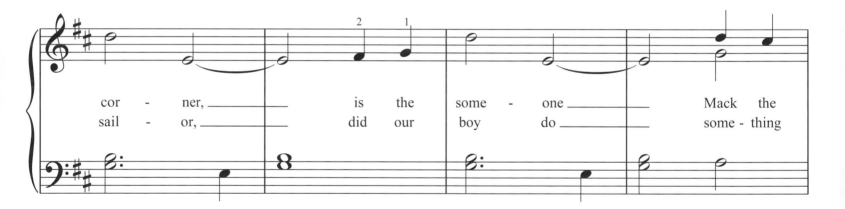

cor - ner, _____ is the some - one _____ Mack the
sail - or, _____ did our boy do _____ some - thing

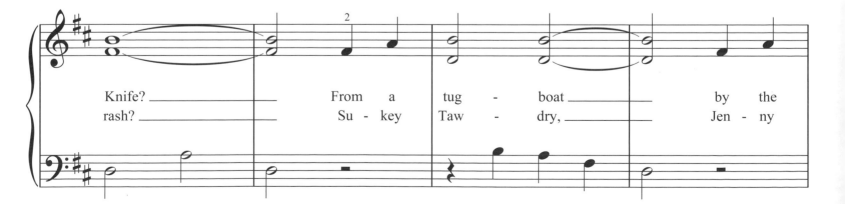

Knife? _____ From a tug - boat _____ by the
rash? _____ Su - key Taw - dry, _____ Jen - ny

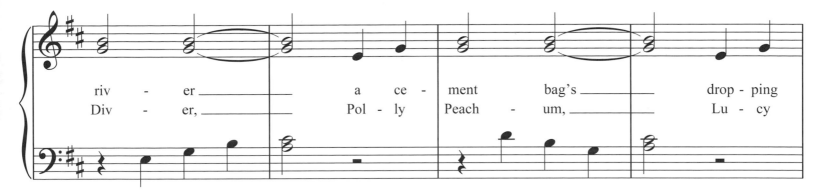

river _____ a ce- ment bag's _____ drop- ping
Div - er, _____ Pol - ly Peach - um, _____ Lu - cy

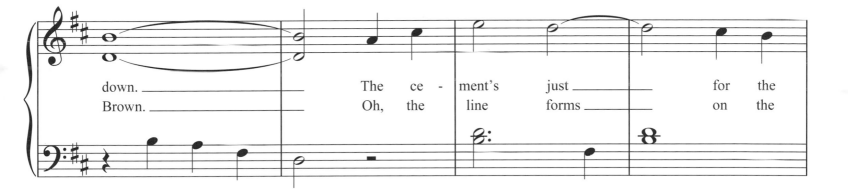

down. _____ The ce- ment's just _____ for the
Brown. _____ Oh, the line just forms _____ on the

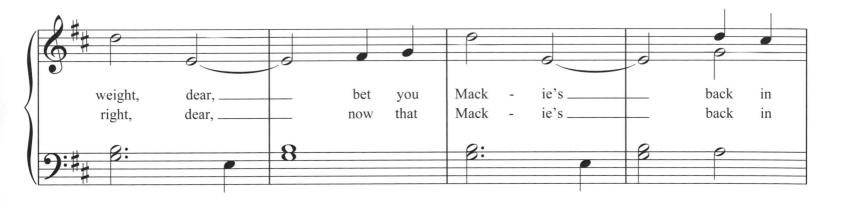

weight, dear, _____ bet you Mack - ie's _____ back in
right, dear, _____ now that Mack - ie's _____ back in

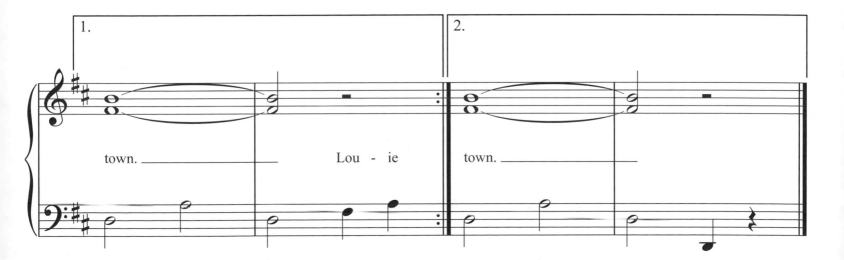

1.
town. _____ Lou - ie

2.
town. _____

MINNIE THE MOOCHER

Words and Music by CAB CALLOWAY
and IRVING MILLS

Moderately slow

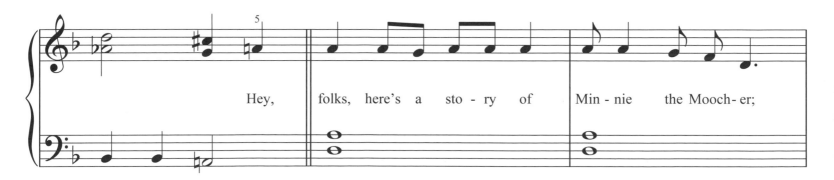

Hey, folks, here's a sto-ry of Min-nie the Mooch-er;

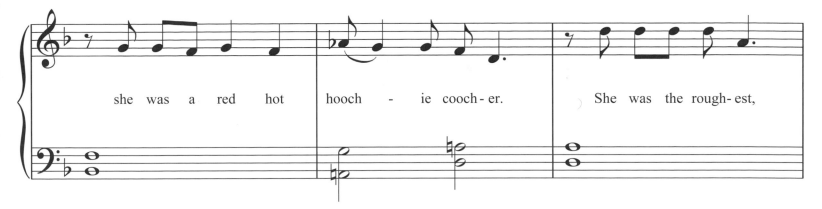

she was a red hot hooch - ie cooch - er. She was the rough-est,

tough-est frail. _ Now, Min - nie had a heart as big as a whale. _ Hi - de

hi - de hi - de hi. (Hi - de hi - de hi - de hi.) Ho - de ho - de ho - de ho. (Ho - de

ho - de ho - de ho.) He - de he - de he - de he. (He - de he - de he - de he.) Hi - de

112

hi - de hi - de hi. (Hi - de hi - de hi - de hi.)

Now she had a dream __ a - bout a

king from Swe - den. He gave her things that she __ was need - in'. Now he

Double Time (♩ = ♩)

built her a home __ of gold and steel __ and a dia - mond car __ with plat - 'num wheels.

Hi - de hi - de hi - de hi - de hi - de hi - de hi. (Hi - de hi - de hi - de hi - de

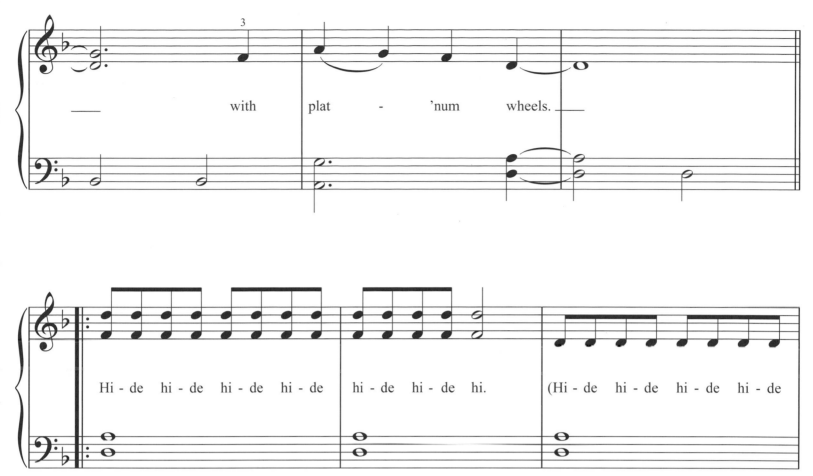

hi - de hi - de hi.) Ho - de ho - de ho - de ho - de ho - de ho - de ho.

Tempo I ($\d = \d$)

(Ho - de ho - de ho - de ho - de ho - de ho - de ho.)

He

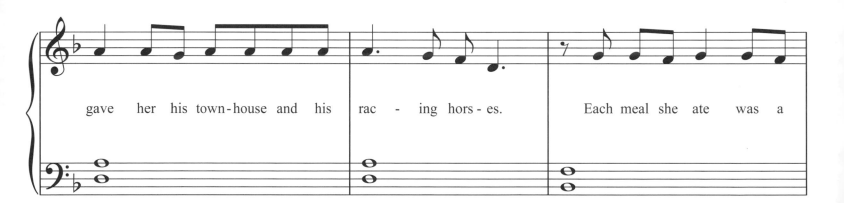

gave her his town-house and his rac - ing hors-es. Each meal she ate was a

doz - en cours-es. She had a mil-lion dol-lars in nick-els and dimes, _ she

sat a - round and count-ed one mil - lion times. ___ Hi - de hi - de hi - de hi. (Hi - de

hi - de - hi - de hi.) Ho - de ho - de ho - de ho. (Ho - de ho - de ho - de ho.) He - de

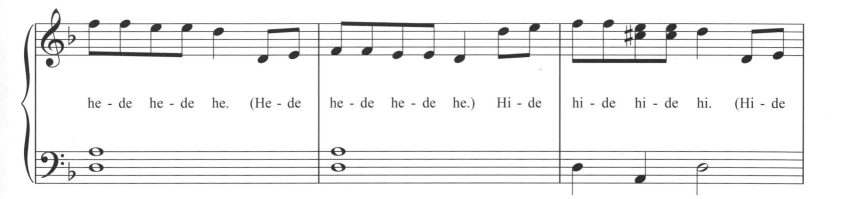

he - de he - de he. (He - de he - de he - de he.) Hi - de hi - de hi - de hi. (Hi - de

Much slower

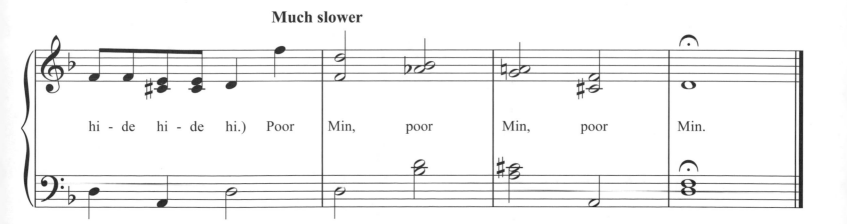

hi - de hi - de hi.) Poor Min, poor Min, poor Min.

MOONLIGHT IN VERMONT

Words by JOHN BLACKBURN
Music by KARL SUESSDORF

Moderately

Pen - nies in a stream, fall - ing leaves, a sy - ca - more,

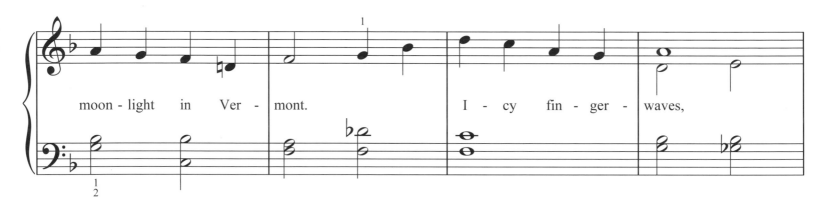

moon - light in Ver - mont. I - cy fin - ger - waves,

ski trails on a moun-tain-side, moon - light in Ver - mont.

Tel - e - graph ca - bles, they sing down the high-way and trav - el each bend ___ in the

road. Peo-ple who meet __ in this ro-man - tic set - ting are

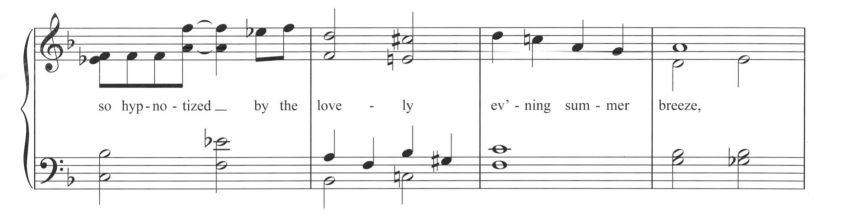

so hyp-no-tized __ by the love - ly ev' - ning sum - mer breeze,

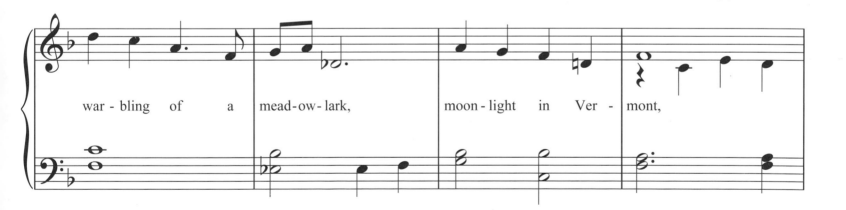

war - bling of a mead-ow-lark, moon-light in Ver - mont,

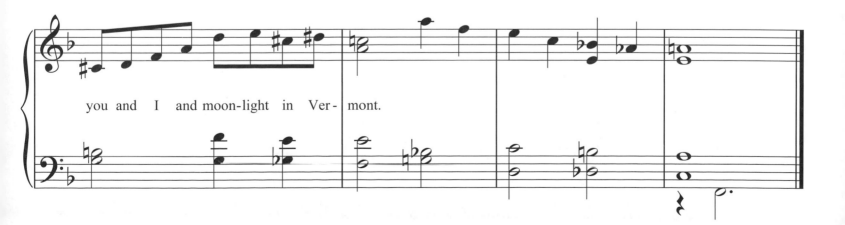

you and I and moon-light in Ver - mont.

THE NEARNESS OF YOU
from the Paramount Picture ROMANCE IN THE DARK

Words by NED WASHINGTON
Music by HOAGY CARMICHAEL

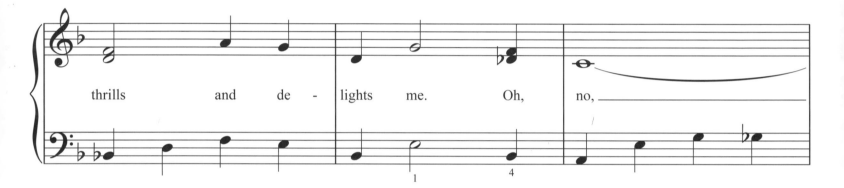

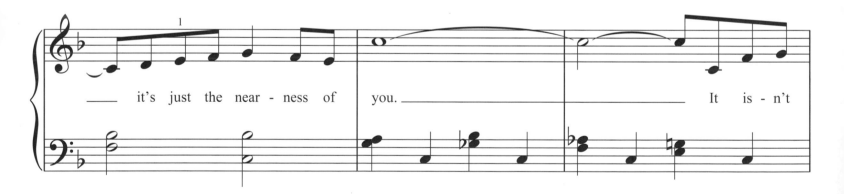

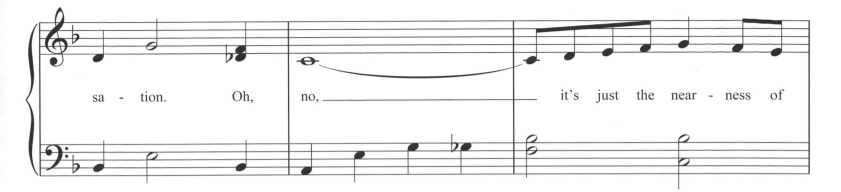

sa - tion.   Oh,   no, _____   it's just the near - ness of

you. _____   When you're in   my   arms _____

___   and   I   feel   you   so   close   to   me, _____   all   my

wild - est   dreams   come   true.   *rit.*   I   need   no

120

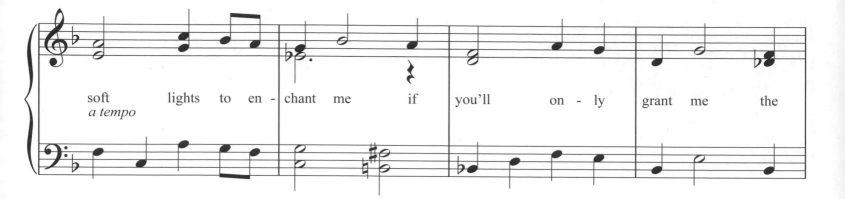

soft   lights to en-chant me   if   you'll   on-ly   grant me   the
a tempo

right _____   to hold you ev-er so tight,

and to feel   in the   night   the   near-ness   of

1.
you. _____   It's not the

2.
you. _____

ONE NOTE SAMBA
(Samba De Uma Nota So)

Original Lyrics by NEWTON MENDONÇA
English Lyrics by ANTONIO CARLOS JOBIM
Music by ANTONIO CARLOS JOBIM

Lightly, with movement

This is just a lit - tle

sam - ba built up - on a sin - gle note. Oth - er notes are bound to

fol - low but the root is still ___ that note. Now the new one is ___ the

con - se - quence of the one we've just ___ been through as I'm bound to be ___ the

un - a - void - a - ble   con - se - quence __ of   you.

There's so man - y peo - ple who can   talk and talk and talk and just say   noth - ing, __ or near - ly

noth - ing. __   I have used up all the scale I   know and at   the end I've come to

noth - ing, __ or near - ly   noth - ing. __ So I   come back to __   my

NIGHT AND DAY
from GAY DIVORCE

Words and Music by
COLE PORTER

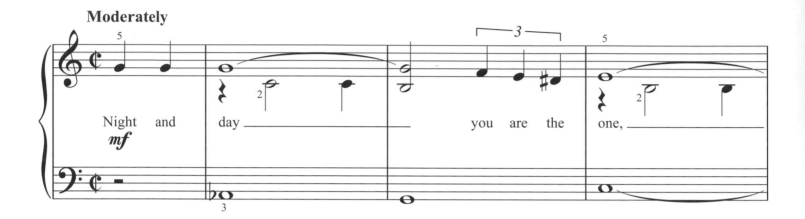

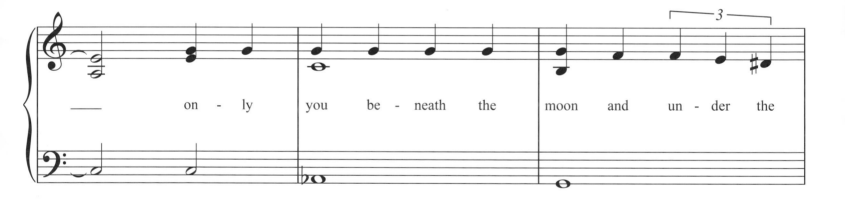

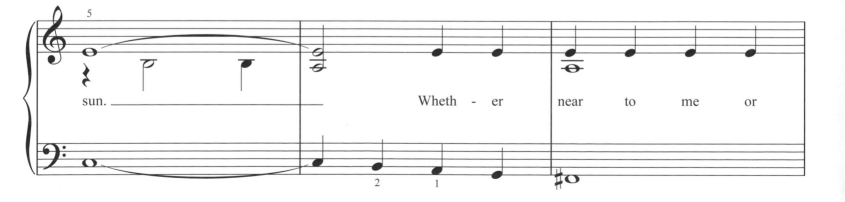

125

far, it's no mat - ter, dar - ling, where you are; I

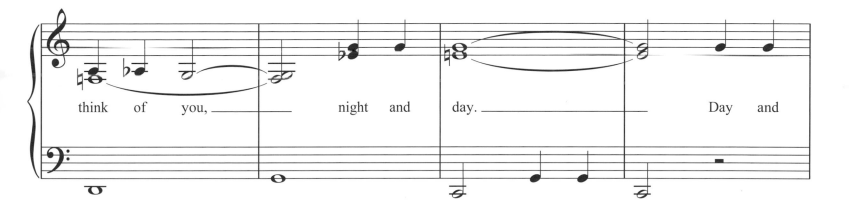

think of you, night and day. Day and

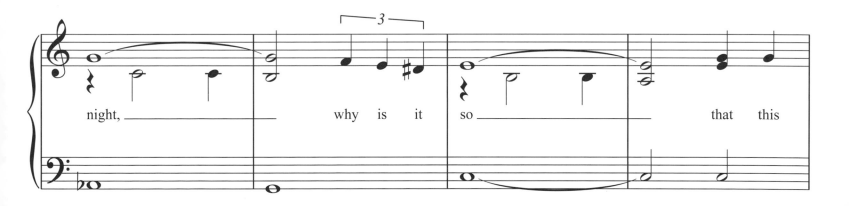

night, why is it so that this

long - ing for you fol - lows wher - ev - er I go?

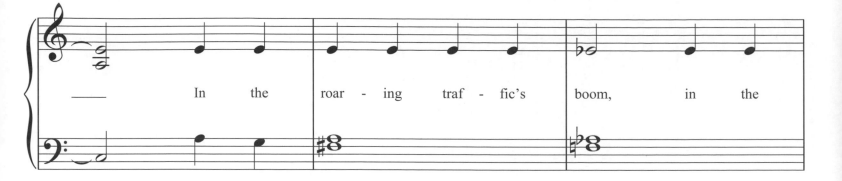

In the roar - ing traf - fic's boom, in the

si - lence of my lone - ly room, I think of you, _____

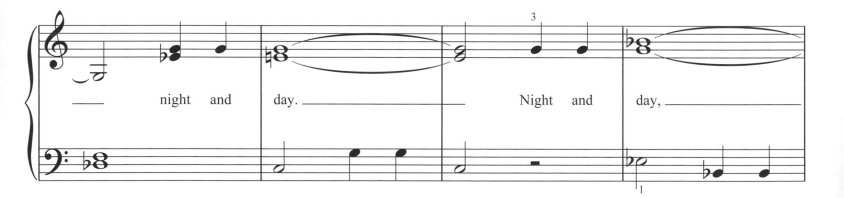

_____ night and day. _____ Night and day, _____

_____ un - der the hide of me _____ there's an,

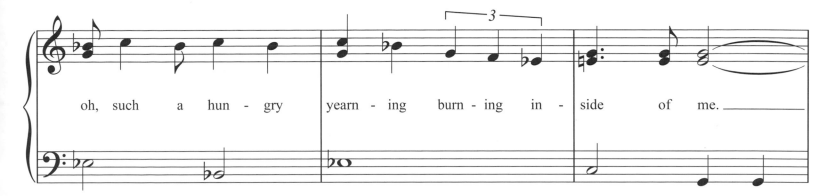

oh, such a hun - gry yearn - ing burn - ing in - side of me.

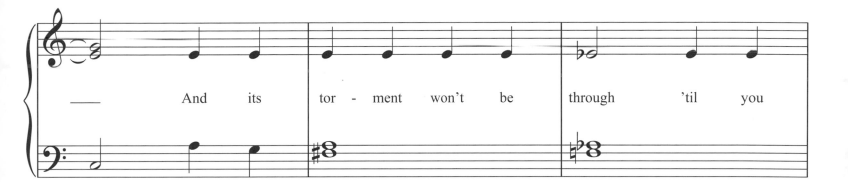

And its tor - ment won't be through 'til you

let me spend my life mak - ing love to you day and night,

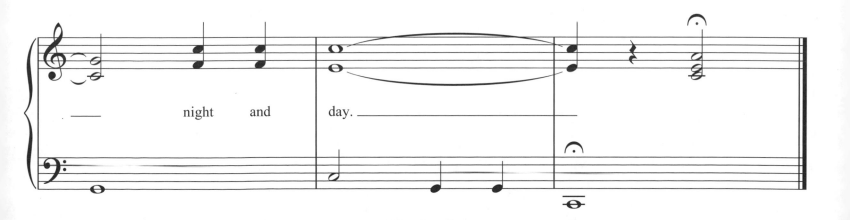

night and day.

NIGHT TRAIN

Words by OSCAR WASHINGTON
and LEWIS C. SIMPKINS
Music by JIMMY FORREST

Medium Swing

To Coda ⊕

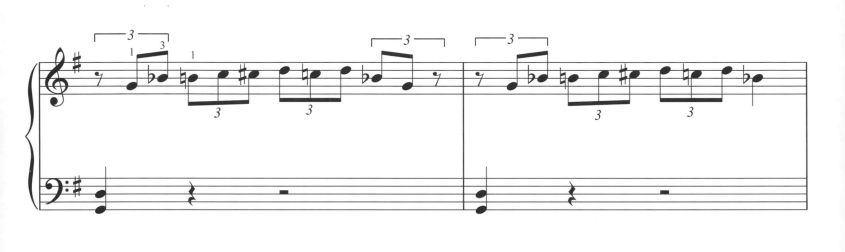

D.C. al Coda

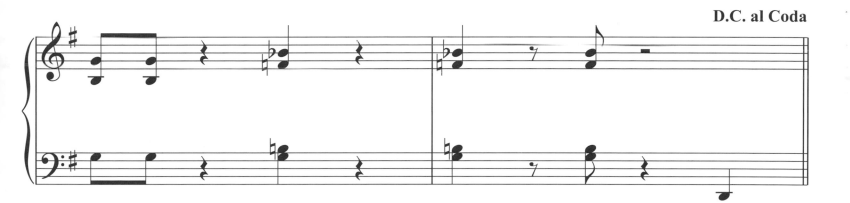

CODA

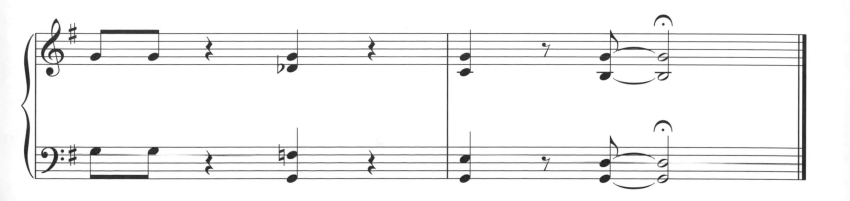

ON GREEN DOLPHIN STREET

Lyrics by NED WASHINGTON
Music by BRONISLAU KAPER

Moderately, with freedom

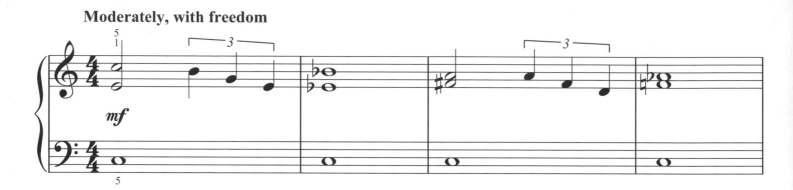

It seems like a dream, yet I know it hap-pened. A

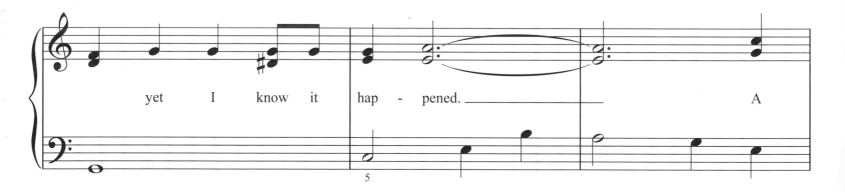

man, a maid, a kiss, and then good-bye.

Ro - mance was the theme, _____ and we were the

play - ers. _____ I nev - er think of this with - out a

A little faster, in tempo

sigh.   *rit.*   Lov   -   er, _____

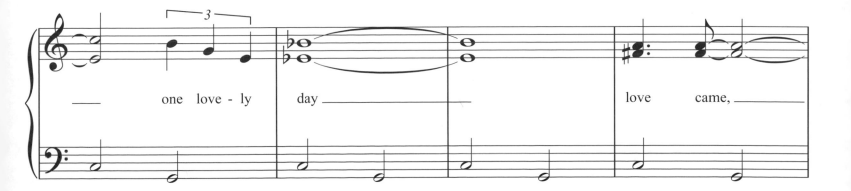

___ one love - ly day _____   love   came, _____

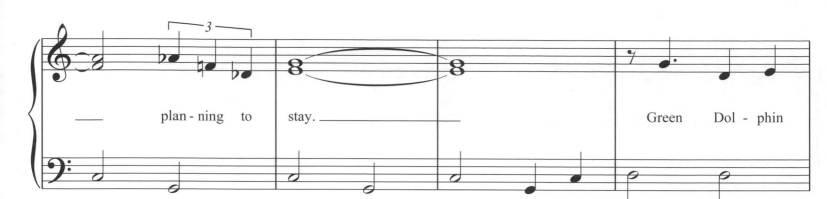

_planning to stay. _____ Green Dol-phin

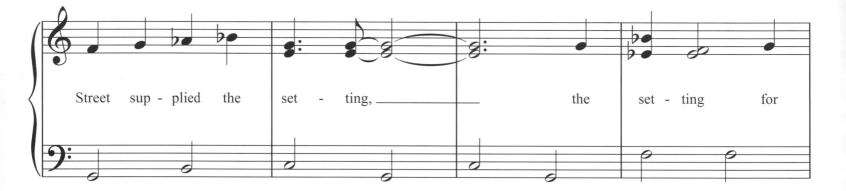

Street sup-plied the set - ting, _____ the set-ting for

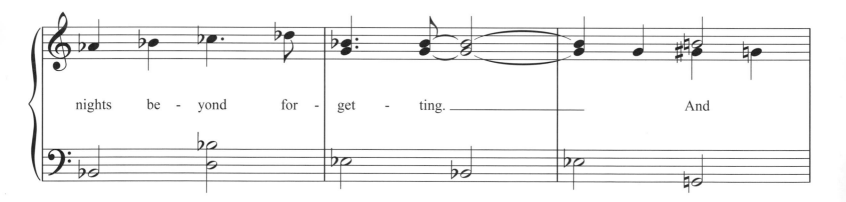

nights be - yond for - get - ting. _____ And

through those _____ mo-ments a - part, _____

mem - 'ries _____ live in my heart. _____

When I re - call the love I found on, ___ I could kiss the

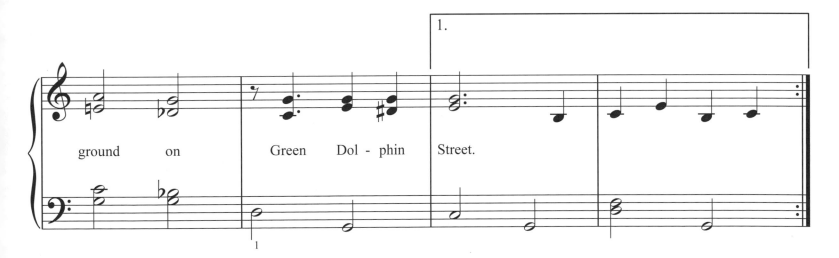

1.

ground on Green Dol - phin Street.

2.

Street. *rit.*

SING, SING, SING

Words and Music by
LOUIS PRIMA

To Coda ⊕   1.

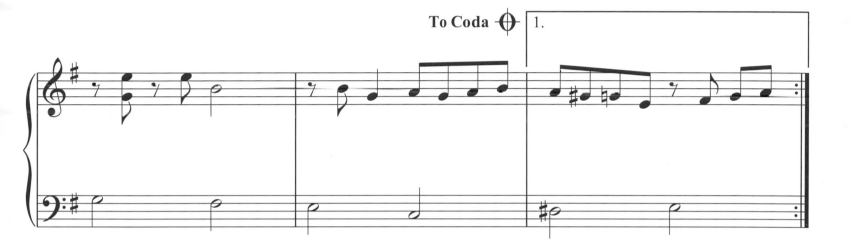

2.

D.S. al Coda

CODA

play RH 2nd time only

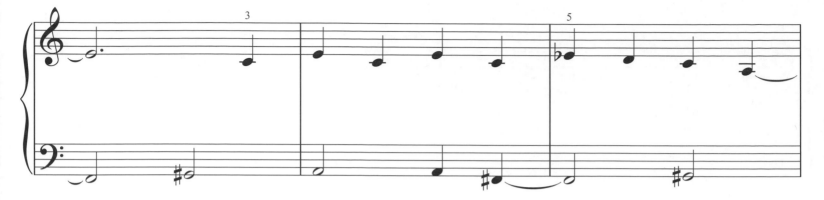

play as written both times

141

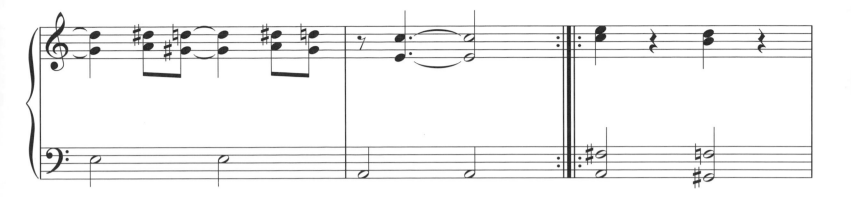

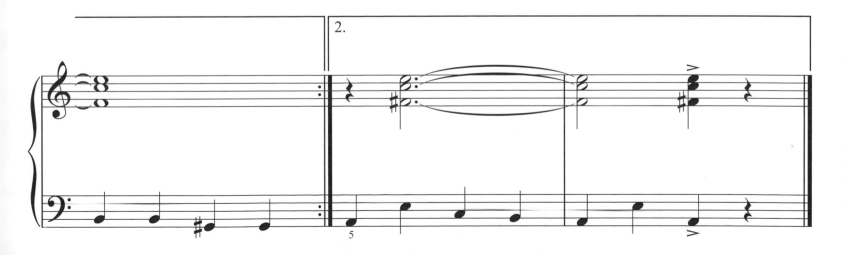

SKYLARK

Words by JOHNNY MERCER
Music by HOAGY CARMICHAEL

green with spring, _____ where my heart can go a - jour - ney - ing _____

_____ o - ver the shad - ows and the rain, to a blos - som - cov - ered lane? And in your

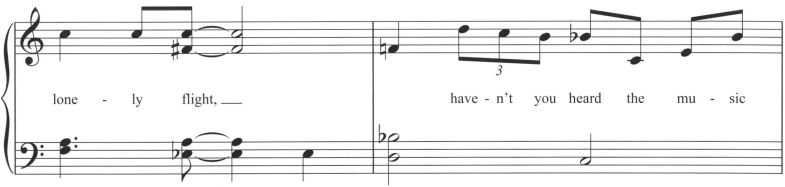

lone - ly flight, _____ have - n't you heard the mu - sic

in the night? __ Won - der - ful mu - sic, faint as a "will - o' - the wisp,"

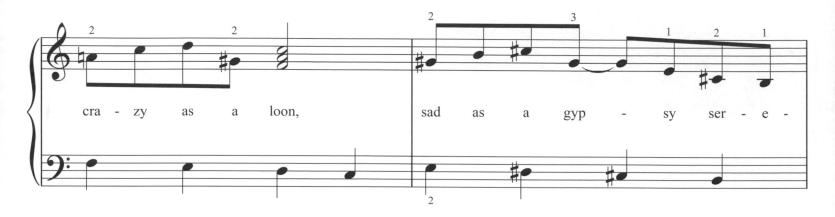

crazy as a loon, sad as a gyp - sy ser - e -

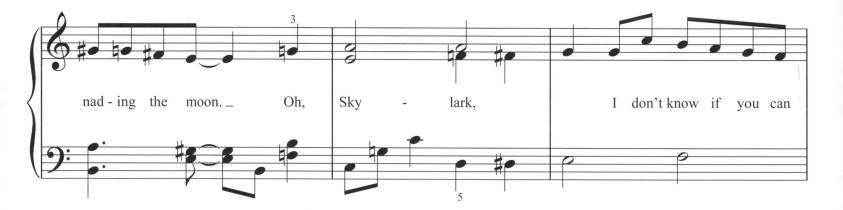

nad - ing the moon. _ Oh, Sky - lark, I don't know if you can

find these things, _ but my heart is rid - ing on your wings. _____

_____ So, if you see them an - y - where, won't you lead me there?

rit.

SO NICE
(Summer Samba)

Original Words and Music by MARCOS VALLE
and PAULO SERGIO VALLE
English Words by NORMAN GIMBEL

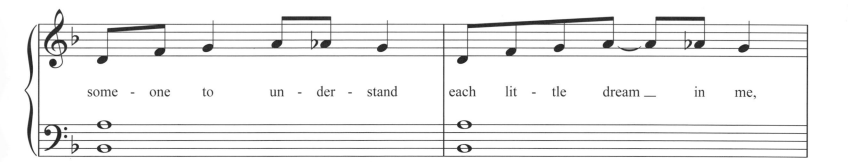

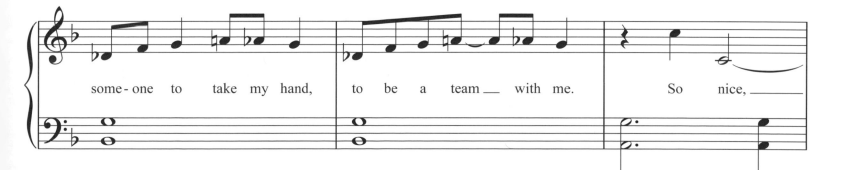

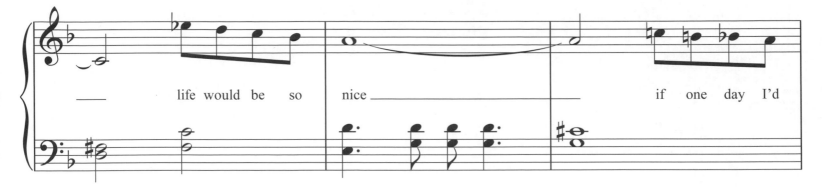

life would be so nice _____ if one day I'd

find _____ some-one who would take my hand and sam-ba through

life with me. Some-one to cling to me, stay with me right __ or wrong,

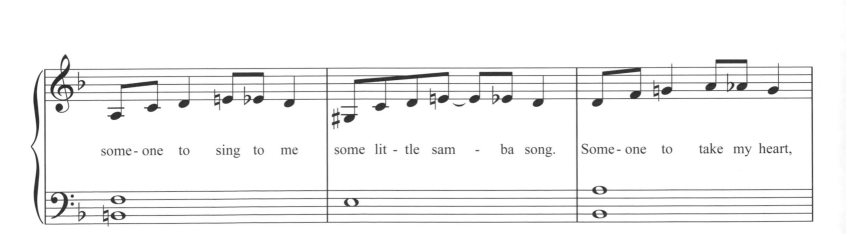

some-one to sing to me some lit-tle sam - ba song. Some-one to take my heart,

then give his heart ___ to me, some-one who's read-y to give love a start ___ with me.

Oh yes, ___ that would be so nice. ___

___ Should it be you and me I could see it would be

1. nice.

2. nice. ___

SWEET GEORGIA BROWN

Words and Music by BEN BERNIE
MACEO PINKARD and KENNETH CASEY

Moderately

No gal made has got a shade on

sweet Geor - gia Brown,_____ two left feet but

oh so neat has sweet Geor - gia Brown._____

They all sigh and wan - na die for sweet Geor - gia Brown, _

_ I'll tell _ you just why, _____ you know _ I don't

lie, not much! It's been said she / All those tips she the

knocks 'em dead when she lands in town; _
por - ter slips to sweet Geor - gia Brown, _

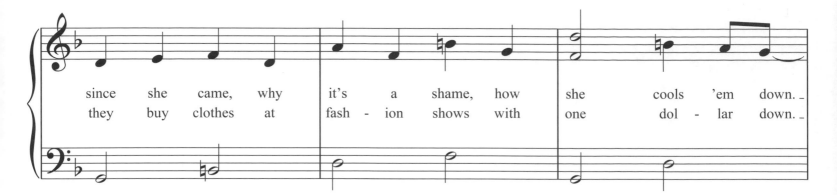

since she came, why | it's a shame, how | she | cools 'em down. _
they buy clothes at | fash - ion shows with | one | dol - lar down. _

___ | Fel - lers ___ | she can't get ___ are
___ | Oh, boy, ___ | tip your hats, _____

fel - lers ___ | she ain't met, ___ | Geor - gia claimed her,
oh, joy, ___ | she's the "cats." _ | Who's that, mis - ter?

Geor - gia named her | sweet Geor - gia | Brown. | Brown.
'Tain't her sis - ter, | sweet Geor - gia |

SOMEONE TO WATCH OVER ME

from OH, KAY!

Music and Lyrics by GEORGE GERSHWIN
and IRA GERSHWIN

Moderately, with a lilt

There's a say-ing old says that love is blind, still we're of-ten told, "Seek and

ye shall find." So I'm going to seek a cer-tain lad I've

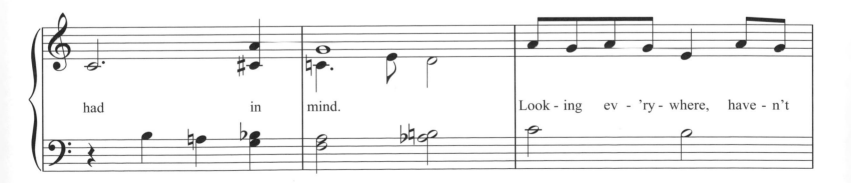

had in mind. Look-ing ev-'ry-where, have-n't

152

found him yet; he's the big af - fair I can - not for - get,

on - ly man I ev - er think of with re - gret.

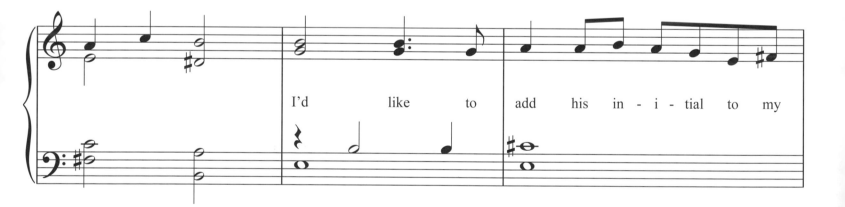

I'd like to add his in - i - tial to my

mon - o - gram. Tell me,

where is the shep-herd for this lost lamb? *rit.*

a tempo There's a some-bod-y I'm long-ing to see. I hope that he

turns out to be some-one who'll watch o - ver

me. I'm a lit - tle lamb who's

154

lost   in   the wood.   I   know   I   could   al - ways   be   good

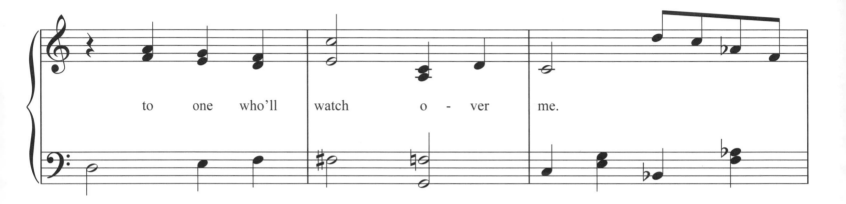

to   one   who'll   watch   o - ver   me.

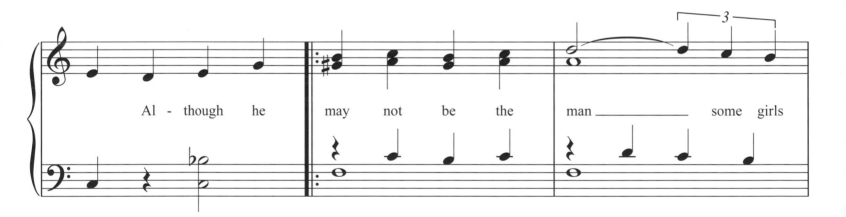

Al - though   he   may   not   be   the   man _____ some   girls

think   of _____   as   hand - some,   to   my   heart   he

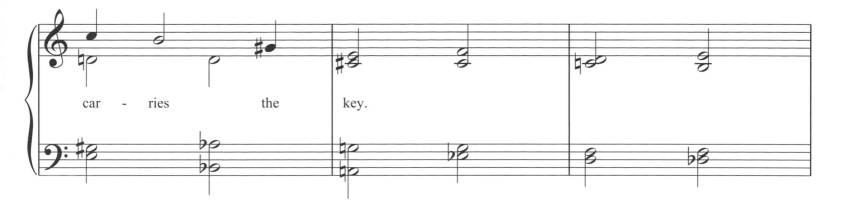

car - ries the key.

Won't you tell him please to put on some speed, fol - low my lead,

oh, how I need some - one to watch o - ver

1. me. Al - though he

2. me. *rit.*

SPRING IS HERE
from I MARRIED AN ANGEL

Words by LORENZ HART
Music by RICHARD RODGERS

Sweetly

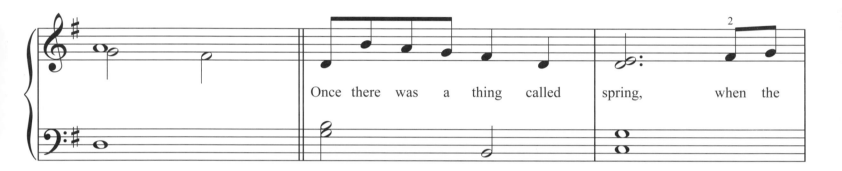

Once there was a thing called spring, when the

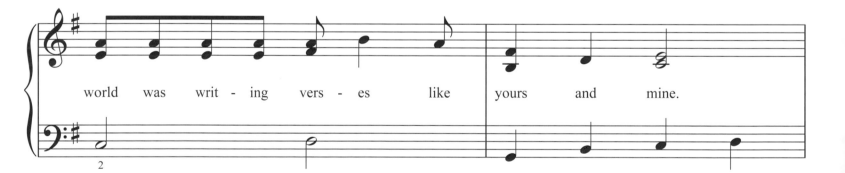

world was writ - ing vers - es like yours and mine.

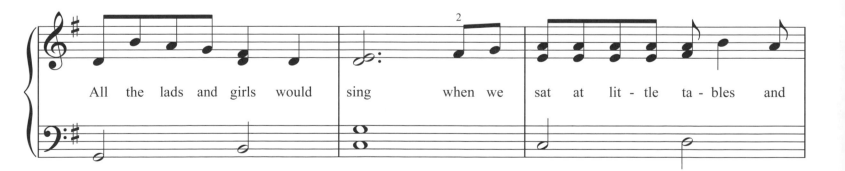

All the lads and girls would sing when we sat at lit - tle ta - bles and

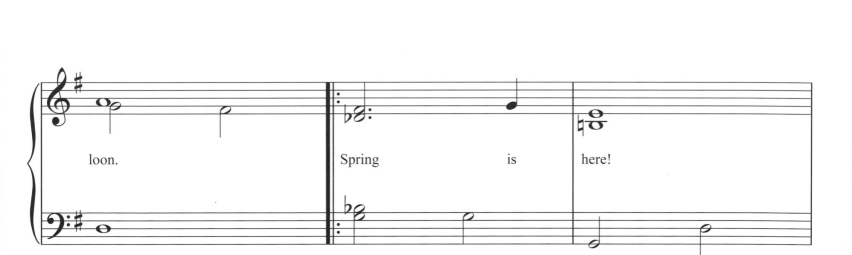

158

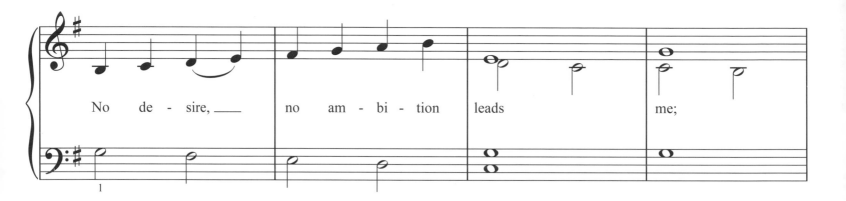

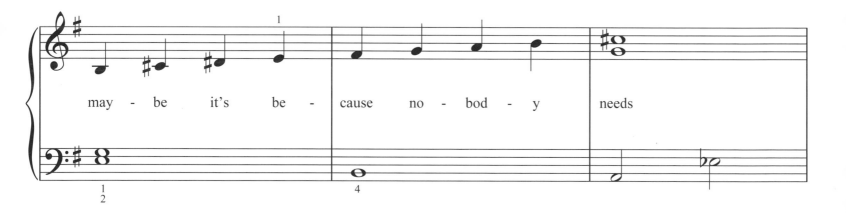

light me? Stars ap - pear. Why does - n't the night in -

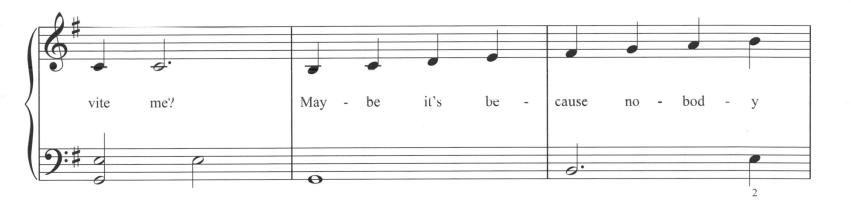

vite me? May - be it's be - cause no - bod - y

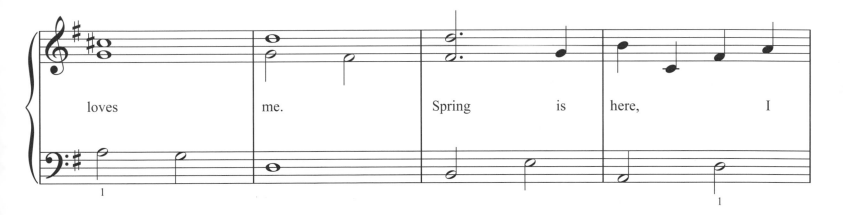

loves me. Spring is here, I

1.
hear!

2.
hear! *rit.*

STARDUST

Words by MITCHELL PARISH
Music by HOAGY CARMICHAEL

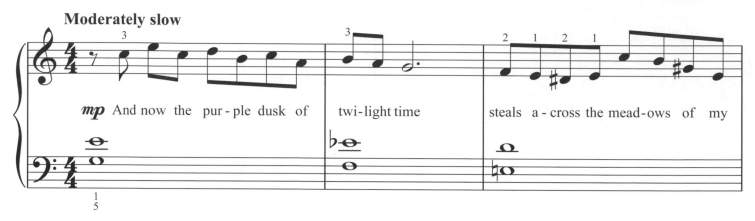

Love is now the star-dust of yes - ter - day, the mu - sic of the years gone

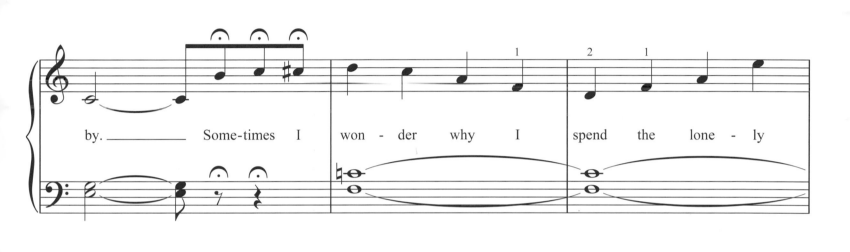

by. _____ Some-times I won - der why I spend the lone - ly

night dream-ing of a song. The mel - o - dy

haunts my rev - e - rie, and I am once a - gain with you, when our

love was new   and each kiss an in - spi - ra - tion. ___

___   But that was long a - go; now my con - sol - a - tion is

in the star - dust of a song.   Be - side a gar - den

wall when stars are bright,   you are in my arms. The

night - in - gale   tells his fair - y tale   of par - a - dise, where ros - es

grew.   Though I dream in vain, _____   in my

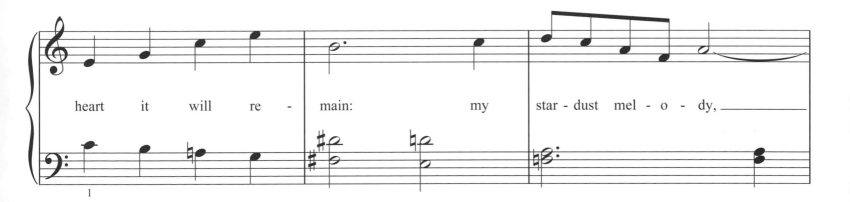

heart it will re - main: my   star - dust mel - o - dy, _____

_____ the mem - o - ry of love's re - frain.
rall.

TAKE FIVE

By PAUL DESMOND

Moderately

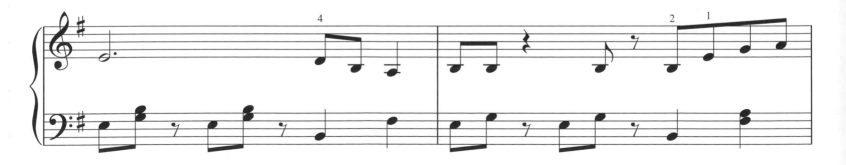

TAKING A CHANCE ON LOVE

from CABIN IN THE SKY

Words by JOHN LA TOUCHE and TED FETTER
Music by VERNON DUKE

Somewhat freely

say, "They're deal-ing you a new hand to-day!" Oh,

Relaxed Shuffle

here I go a - gain. ___
Here I come a - gain. ___
Here I slip a - gain, ___

I hear those trum - pets
I'm gon - na make things
a - bout to take that

blow a - gain, ___
hum a - gain. ___
tip a - gain. ___

all a - glow a - gain, ___
Act - ing dumb a - gain, ___
Got my grip a - gain, ___

tak - ing a chance on love.
tak - ing a chance on love.
tak - ing a chance on love.

Here I
Here I I
Now I I

170

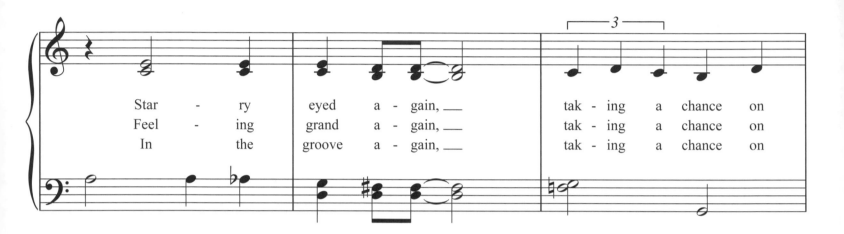

game up _____ and the | ace of hearts is | high.
num - bers _____ on a | lit - tle dream for | two.
course, you _____ bet - ter | kiss your foot good - | bye.

Things are | mend - ing now; ___ | I see a rain - bow
Wad - ing | in a - gain, ___ | I'm lead - in' with my
On the | ball a - gain, ___ | I'm rid - in' for a

blend - ing now. ___ | We'll have our hap - py | end - ing now, ___
chin a - gain. ___ | I'm start - in' out to | win a - gain, ___
fall a - gain. ___ | I'm gon - na give my | all a - gain, ___

tak - ing a chance on | love.
tak - ing a chance on | love.
tak - ing a chance on | love.

THE VERY THOUGHT OF YOU

Words and Music by
RAY NOBLE

Moderately slow

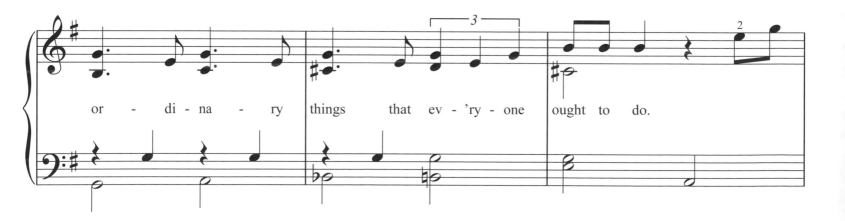

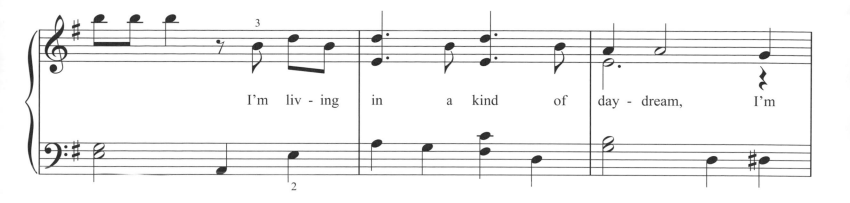

I'm liv - ing in a kind of day - dream, I'm

hap - py as a king, and fool - ish though it

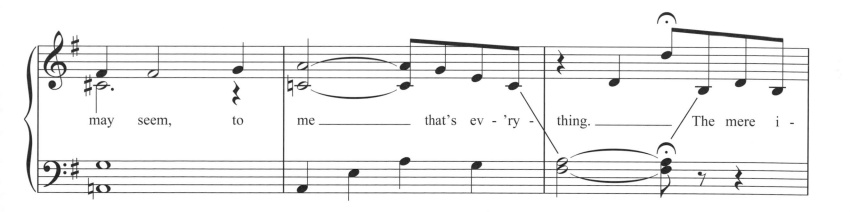

may seem, to me _____ that's ev - 'ry - thing. _____ The mere i -

dea of you, the long - ing here for you,

174

you'll nev - er know how slow the mo -- ments go 'til I'm

near to you. I see your face in ev - 'ry flow - er, your

eyes in stars a - bove. _____ It's just the thought of you, ___ the ver - y

rit. *a tempo*

thought of you, my love.

rit.

YOU AND THE NIGHT AND THE MUSIC

from REVENGE WITH MUSIC

Words by HOWARD DIETZ
Music by ARTHUR SCHWARTZ

Dramatically, with freedom

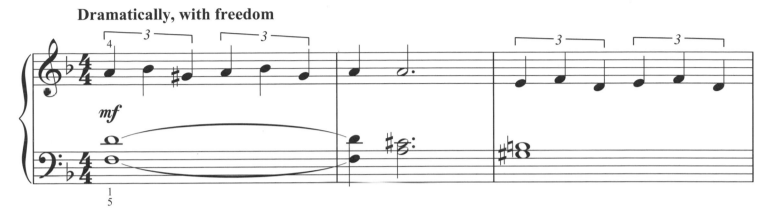

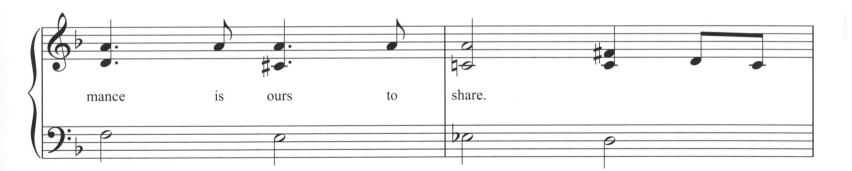

176

lone.

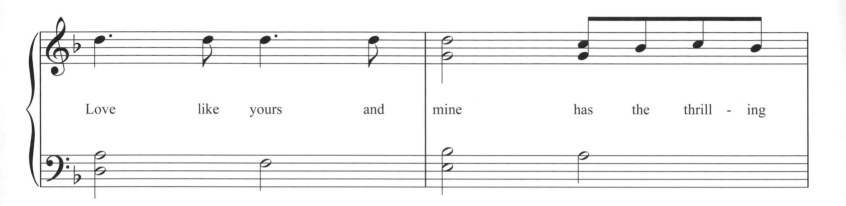

Love   like   yours   and   mine   has   the   thrill - ing

glow   of   a   spark - ling   wine,   make   the   most   of

time   ere   it   has   flown. _____   *rall.*

Easy Latin feel

You and the night and the mu - sic

a tempo

fill me with flam - ing de - sire, set - ting my be - ing com -

plete - ly on fire!

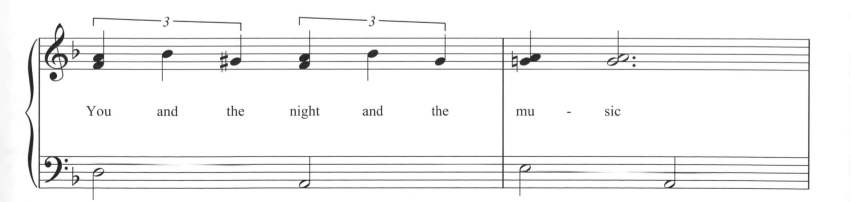

You and the night and the mu - sic

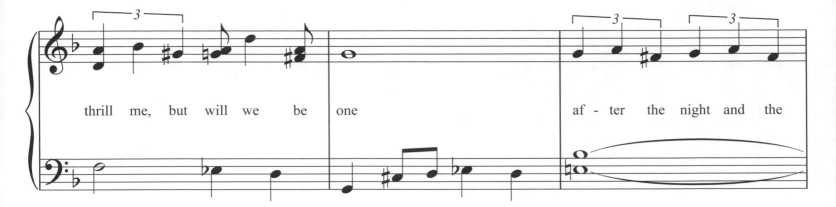

thrill me, but will we be one af - ter the night and the

mu - sic are done? _____ Un - til the

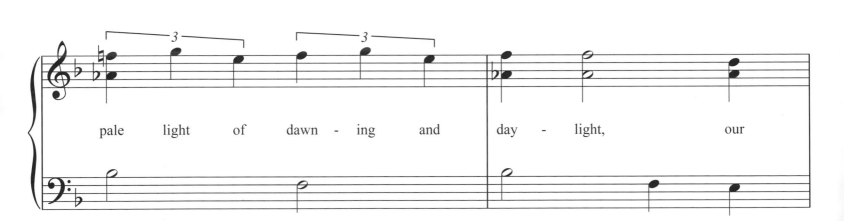

pale light of dawn - ing and day - light, our

hearts will be throb - bing gui - tars. Morn - ing may come with - out

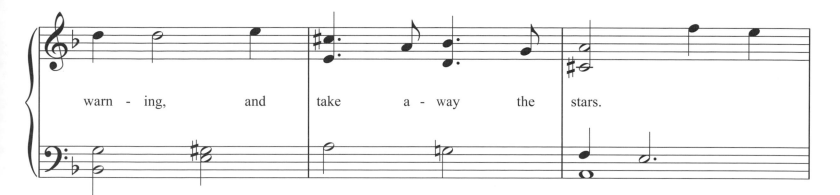

warn - ing, and take a - way the stars.

If we must live for the mo - ment, love till the mo - ment is

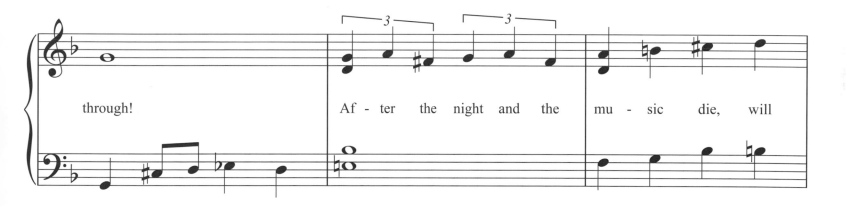

through! Af - ter the night and the mu - sic die, will

I have you? you?

YESTERDAYS
from ROBERTA

Words by OTTO HARBACH
Music by JEROME KERN

Moderately slow, in 2

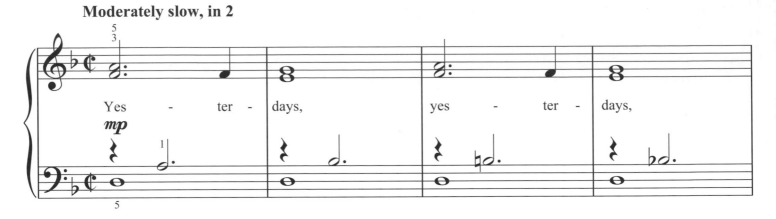

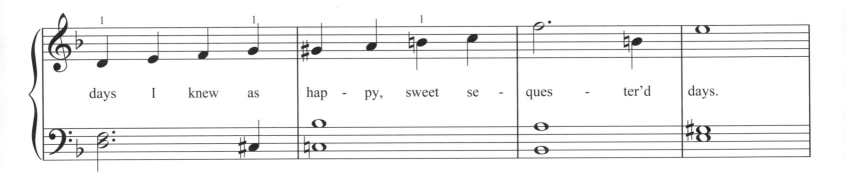

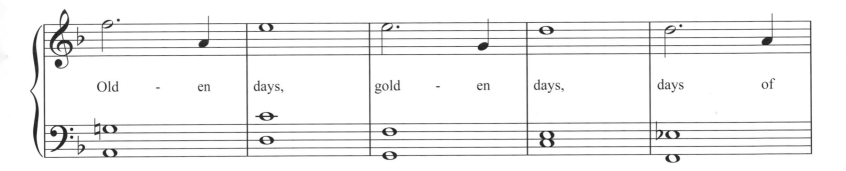

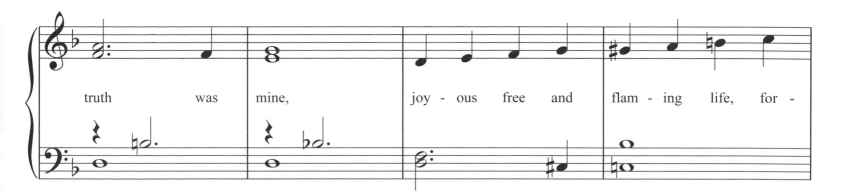

truth was mine, joy - ous free and flam - ing life, for -

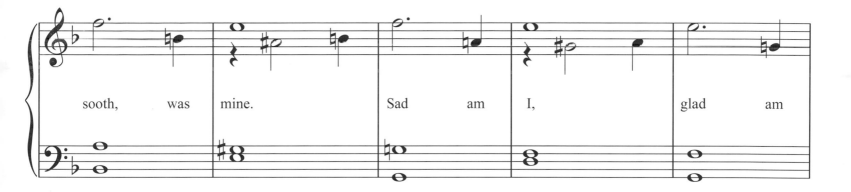

sooth, was mine. Sad am I, glad am

I, for to - day I'm dream - ing of yes - ter -

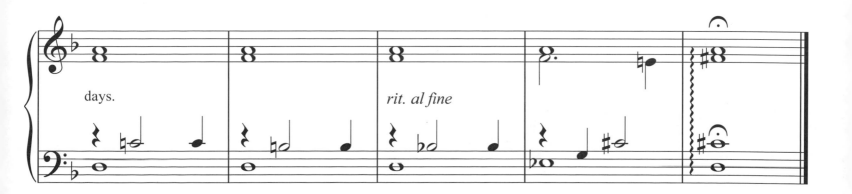

days. *rit. al fine*

YOU ARE TOO BEAUTIFUL

from HALLELUJAH, I'M A BUM

Words by LORENZ HART
Music by RICHARD RODGERS

one luck-y fool to be with, when there are oth-er men with

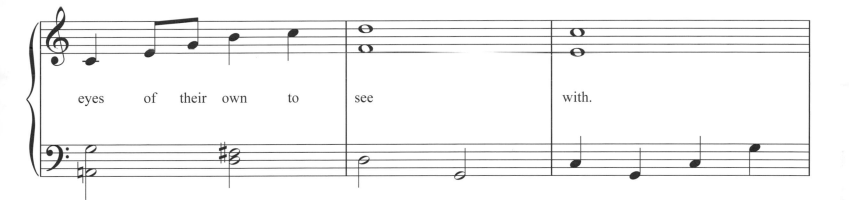

eyes of their own to see with.

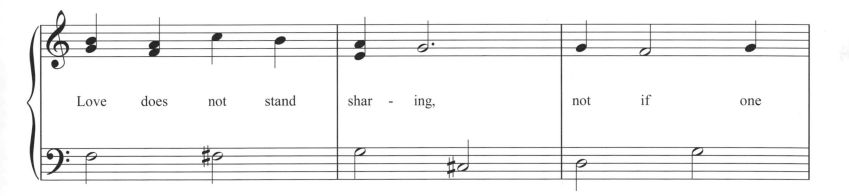

Love does not stand shar - ing, not if one

cares. Have you been com - par - ing

my ev - 'ry kiss with theirs? If, on the oth - er hand, I'm

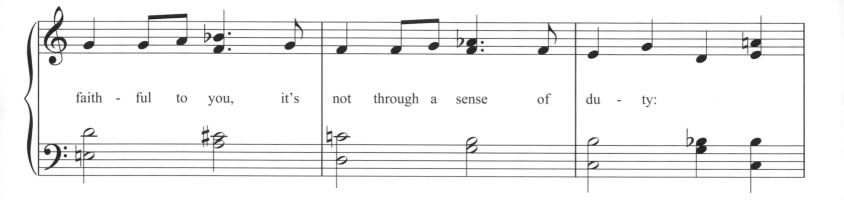

faith - ful to you, it's not through a sense of du - ty:

You are too beau - ti - ful and I am a fool for beau -

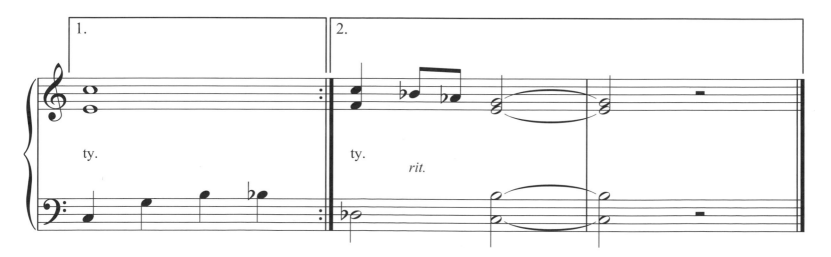

1.

ty.

2.

ty.

rit.

YOU'D BE SO NICE TO COME HOME TO

from SOMETHING TO SHOUT ABOUT

Words and Music by
COLE PORTER

Slowly and expressively

You'd be so nice to come home to, you'd be so

nice by the fire, while the

breeze, on high, _____ sang a lull - a -

by, _____ you'd be all that I could de -

sire. _____ Un - der stars,

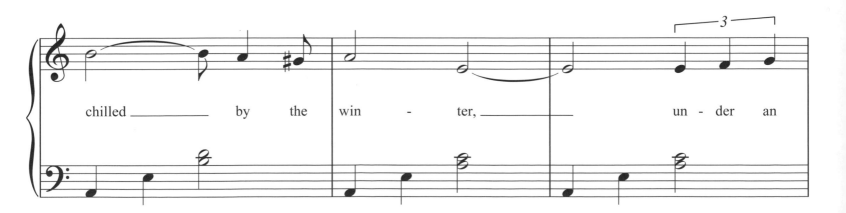

chilled _____ by the win - ter, _____ un - der an

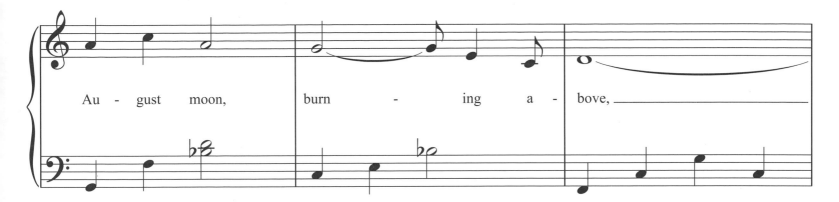

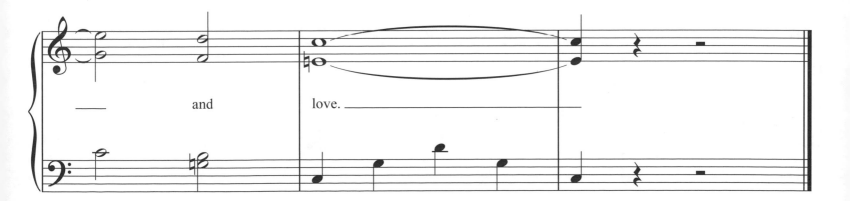

YOU DON'T KNOW WHAT LOVE IS

Words and Music by DON RAYE
and GENE De PAUL

Slowly

You don't know ____ what

love is ____ un - til you've learned the mean - ing of the

blues; un - til you've loved a love you've had to

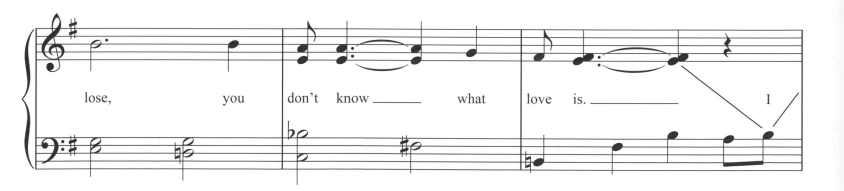

lose, you don't know ____ what love is. ____ I

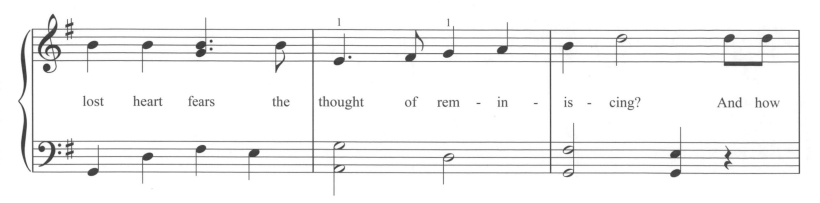

lost   heart   fears   the   thought   of   rem - in - is - cing?   And how

lips   that taste   of   tears   lose   their   taste   for

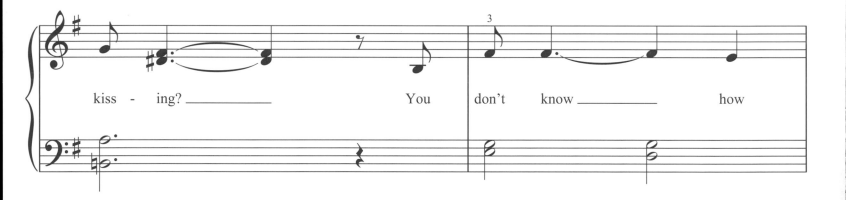

kiss - ing? _____   You   don't   know _____   how

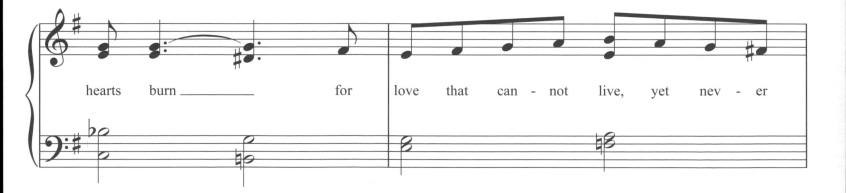

hearts   burn _____   for   love   that   can - not   live,   yet   nev - er

dies.   Un - til you've faced each dawn with sleep - less

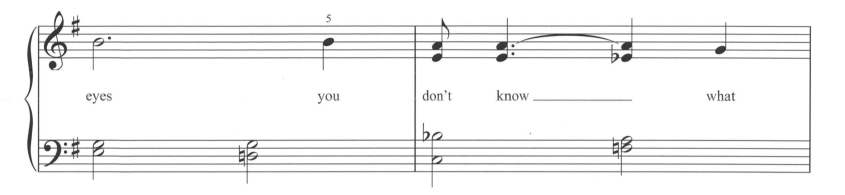

eyes   you   don't know _____ what

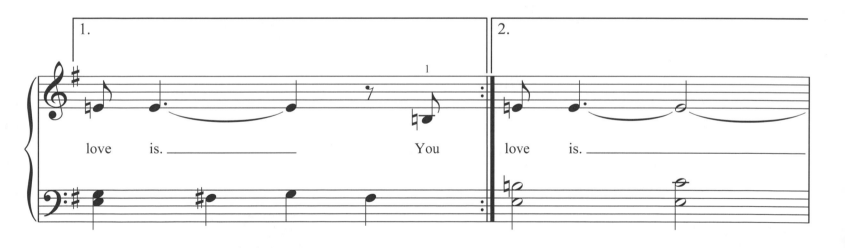

1.

love is. _____ You

2.

love is. _____

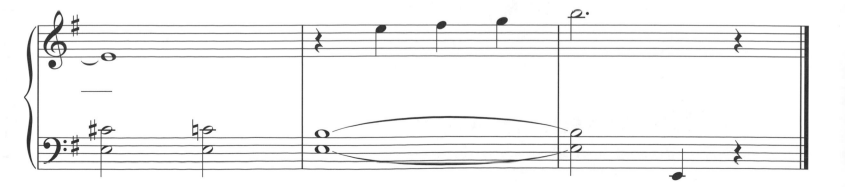

SIMPLE SONGS

THE TITLE SAYS IT ALL: The easiest easy piano arrangements with lyrics to make even beginners sound great! Songs in each collection are carefully chosen to work in these streamlined arrangements.

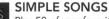

SIMPLE SONGS

Play 50 of your favorite songs in the easiest of arrangements! Enjoy pop hits, Broadway showstoppers, movie themes, jazz standards, folk tunes and classical melodies presented simply, with lyrics. You'll find something for everyone! Songs include: Beyond the Sea • Castle on a Cloud • Do-Re-Mi • Happy Birthday to You • Hey Jude • Let It Go • Linus and Lucy • Moon River • Ode to Joy • Over the Rainbow • Puff the Magic Dragon • Smile • Star Wars (Main Theme) • Tomorrow • When I Fall in Love • Yesterday • and more.

00142041.. $16.99

(MORE) SIMPLE SONGS

The first edition of our "easiest of easy piano songs" collection was such a success that we found 50 more favorite songs in the easiest of arrangements presented simply, with lyrics. Songs include: All of Me • Brave • Crazy • Danny Boy • Edelweiss • Für Elise • Hallelujah • It's a Small World • Lean on Me • Music Box Dancer • The Pink Panther • Sing • This Land Is Your Land • Unchained Melody • You Raise Me Up • and more.

00172308.. $16.99

SIMPLE BROADWAY SONGS

Play 50 of your favorite songs in the easiest of arrangements! Enjoy Broadway show-stoppers presented simply, with lyrics. You'll find something for everyone! Songs include: Dancing Queen · Defying Gravity · Edelweiss · Let It Go · Mama, I'm a Big Girl Now · My Shot · The Music of the Night · Puttin' on the Ritz · Seasons of Love · When I Grow Up · And more!

00295064.. $16.99

SIMPLE CHRISTMAS CAROLS

Play 50 classic carols in the easiest of arrangements, presented simply, with lyrics. Includes: Away in a Manger • Deck the Hall • The First Noel • Go, Tell It on the Mountain • Hark! The Herald Angels Sing • It Came upon the Midnight Clear • Jingle Bells • O Holy Night • Silent Night • The Twelve Days of Christmas • What Child Is This? • and more.

00278263.. $14.99

SIMPLE CHRISTMAS SONGS

Play 50 well-loved holiday songs in the easiest of arrangements! Enjoy classic and contemporary favorites presented simply, with lyrics. Songs include: All I Want for Christmas Is My Two Front Teeth • Blue Christmas • Christmas Time Is Here • Feliz Navidad • Grandma Got Run over by a Reindeer • Have Yourself a Merry Little Christmas • It's Beginning to Look like Christmas • Jingle Bell Rock • Let It Snow! Let It Snow! Let It Snow! • The Most Wonderful Time of the Year • Nuttin' for Christmas • Rudolph the Red-Nosed Reindeer • Santa Claus Is Comin' to Town • Winter Wonderland • You're All I Want for Christmas • and more.

00237197.. $16.99

SIMPLE CLASSICAL PIANO PIECES

Play 50 favorites by Bach, Beethoven, Mozart and others that are perfect for beginners. Pieces include: Minuet in G Major, BWV Appendix 116 • Arabesque from *25 Progressive Studies*, Op. 100, No. 2 • Aria in D minor • Russian Song from *Album for the Young*, Op. 39, No. 11 • Dance in G Major • and more.

00288045.. $9.99

SIMPLE DISNEY SONGS

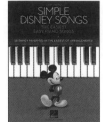

Play 50 favorite Disney songs in the easiest of arrangements! Enjoy these classic and contemporary selections presented simply, with lyrics. Songs include: Almost There • The Bare Necessities • I've Got a Dream • If I Didn't Have You • Just Around the Riverbend • Let's Go Fly a Kite • Love Is an Open Door • Once upon a Dream • Reflection • Seize the Day • Under the Sea • When You Wish upon a Star • and more.

00355319.. $19.99

Disney characters and artwork (c) & TM 2021 Disney

SIMPLE JAZZ SONGS

Play 50 of your favorite songs in the easiest of arrangements! Enjoy jazz standards presented simply, with lyrics. You'll find something for everyone! Songs include: As Time Goes By • Blue Moon • Here's That Rainy Day • It Had to Be You • Love Is Here to Stay • Mack the Knife • The Nearness of You • On Green Dolphin Street • Sing, Sing, Sing • Someone to Watch Over Me • Sweet Georgia Brown • You'd Be So Nice to Come Home To • and more.

00355461.. $19.99

SIMPLE MOVIE SONGS

Play 50 favorite movie songs in the easiest of arrangements! Enjoy songs from a variety of genres presented simply in easy piano arrangements with lyrics. Includes: Born Free • Cups (When I'm Gone) (from *Pitch Perfect*) • Dawn (from *Pride & Prejudice*) • Endless Love • Gabriel's Oboe (from *The Mission*) • If I Only Had a Brain (from *The Wizard of Oz*) • James Bond Theme • A Million Dreams (from *The Greatest Showman*) • Theme from New York, New York • The Pink Panther • Shallow (from *A Star Is Born*) • Time Warp (from *Rocky Horror Picture Show*) • and many more.

00295065.. $16.99

Browse more products and order today from your favorite music retailer at
halleonard.com

Prices, contents and availability subject to change without notice.